BREAKING
THE CHAINS

The Bundle of Sticks

"You have all heard of the foolish old woman who went out and bought a bundle of sticks tied tightly together with a piece of string. She was in a hurry to get the fire lit when she came home, so she tried to break the bundle as it was. What was the result? She did not break the sticks. She nearly broke her fingers instead. Had she untied the string, each stick could easily have been broken separately, but united together the sticks protected each other, and could not be broken.

A Trade Union is like a bundle of sticks. The workers are bound together and have the strength of unity. No employer can do as he likes with them. They have the power of resistance. They can ask for an advance without fear. A worker who is not in the Union is like a single stick. She can easily be broken or bent to the will of her employer. She has not power to resist a reduction in wages. If she is fined, she must pay without complaint. She dare not ask for a 'rise'. If she does she will be told, "Your place is outside the gate; there are plenty to take your place." An employer can do without one worker. He cannot do without all his workers. If all the workers united in a Union – strong as the bundle of sticks – complain or ask for improved conditions, the employer is bound to listened."

(Mary Reid Macarthur – 1907)

*   *   *   *   *

This book is dedicated to all of the women of Cradley Heath, whose courage and conviction to stand up and be heard, gave opportunities to millions of others living hopeless lives.

"Extreme hopes are born of extreme misery."

Bertrand Russell

BREAKING THE CHAINS

The story of the women chainmakers from Cradley Heath

Jean Debney

BREWIN BOOKS

First published by
Brewin Books Ltd, 56 Alcester Road,
Studley, Warwickshire B80 7LG in 2010
www.brewinbooks.com

ISBN: 978-1-85858-470-6

A Cataloguing in Publication Record
for this title is available from the British Library.

Typeset in New Baskerville
Printed in Great Britain by
Information Press Ltd.

TABLE OF CONTENTS

	Foreword	vii
	Introduction	ix
1	The Melting Pot of Change	1
2	Where there's Muck, there's Money	10
3	A Woman's Work?	20
4	In Chains	31
5	Those that tried to make a Difference	40
6	Mary Reid Macarthur	54
7	By the Sweat of their Brow	66
8	The Trade Off	77
9	The 'Lock Out'	89
10	United we stand together	100
11	The Aftermath	112
12	Conclusions	123

Appendices

I	The Song of the Shirt – Thomas Hood	130
II	Rebecca, Stories of Chain making – Yvonne Routledge	133
III	The Home-Life of the Sweated – George Haw	136
IV	Songs from the Cradley Heath Chainmakers' Strike of 1910	138
V	The Procession – John Galsworthy	140
	Bibliography	144

ACKNOWLEDGEMENTS

I would like to give my thanks to the family of Mary Macarthur, in particular, her grandson James Crawford Bargrave Deane, for all of his support towards this project. Additionally, Mrs C. Coates at the TUC Archive for her expertise and direction and The Black Country Living Museum for the release of images for this book.

FOREWORD
by Charles Allen CBE

I have had many influences in both my personal life and my career but passion, tenacity, the importance of equality and diversity, the influence of strong women and the need to manage change have played a key role in shaping my path. This book captures the essence of these influences and tells a powerful story of compassionate people with the will to change society for the better.

In the modern world, the management of change is a carefully analysed and well-documented process. Within my own experience it is a process that leads to improvement of any system and industry, but will always carry the inherent difficulties of customary tradition/dogma and resentment of the 'new'. My reading of this book by Doctor Debney highlights that these necessary and sometimes painful processes are nothing new and in fact, many were emerging at this particular point in history.

There are many significant parallels in the Edwardian Industrial society with present day experience and much of that has subsequently been put into practice. In all probability, this is a direct consequence of the wave of social philanthropy that developed at that time.

As she has correctly analysed, no one event or person can be identified as the ultimate catalyst for any significant change; that is as true now as ever, it is combination of circumstances and people that creates the melee, the thrust for dynamic transition towards a more efficient and effective organisation. In any of these examples, which she examines in her text, whether it be the national, social or industrial perspectives, one can easily identify the 'enablers' and 'resistors' towards the new, to use the modern jargon.

From my understanding of what she has thoroughly researched and précised, this was indeed a pivotal moment in the establishment of the modern industrial age. Society was moving from an established status quo in all aspects and at great speed, being met by the needs to recognise the value of each individual within the structure of that society. Much of this was due to the emerging middle class, many of whom had created their own position through their newly acquired industrial wealth. It is interesting to note that the likes of Edward Cadbury took his position as an industrial philanthropist particularly seriously, and used his research and knowledge to inform those with similar backgrounds and interests.

Trade Unionism in this present world does not always rest with Industry as comfortable bed fellows and it is clear from what I have read here, that indeed they never were; however, what was achieved then was not only critical to the local and national perspectives of that time, but essential for the wealth creation subsequently generated by their persuasive intrusions into unfair working practices that existed at that time. Without the remarkable efforts of the NFWW led by the most able Mary Macarthur et al, there would not have been the wave of change that granted the rights to all workers for a 'living wage'.

I am a great believer that each individual plays an important part in any organisation or structure. It is a foolish leader who undervalues those of any level within their sphere of practice. This book is a great leveller to all of us in the modern world, and provokes deep thought about exactly how far we have come in achieving an equitable and equal society presently. Many lessons are learnt through the study of history, and as Jean Debney carefully articulates, there is nothing new that has not been experienced at sometime in the past. To me this book brings us full circle and is a 'must read' for all those concerned with all aspects of growing economies and wealth creation, for only by placing value on the microcosm of society can we truly build strength.

Charles L Allen CBE
Broadcaster and Businessman

INTRODUCTION

In October 1910 one of the most significant achievements in Trade Union history came to pass, this happening brought about the settlement of the first ever legally agreed minimum wage for any trade. The event in question was the ending of a ten week lock-out of the women chainmakers of a little town in the Black Country called Cradley Heath. This year will mark the centenary of that victory of the strikers and coincides with the commencement of the period which we now know as the 'Great Unrest'; the years when there was a general uprising of the downtrodden working class in order to achieve that same desire – a living wage.

This book aims to frame that event in its true context; politically and socially, locally and nationally. I will endeavour to balance all the aspects that produced the groundswell of a movement for change across what in our history was a relatively short period of time. You will be introduced to the key figures of influence who made the victory possible, including Sir Charles Dilke MP and his wife Lady Emilia, aided and abetted by her niece Gertrude Tuckwell, James Joseph Mallon, who was instrumental in the establishment of the National Anti-Sweating League, Mr Thomas Sitch and his son Charles, who led the Chainmakers' Strikers' Association and the Cradley Heath branch of the NFWW respectively, Julia Varley who was the regional organiser for the NFWW and a staunch trade unionist, and the one most credited with that victory – the redoubtable Mary Reid Macarthur.

I will endeavour to paint a picture of life in Edwardian England, the changes that were impacting upon society with the emerging middle class and their interest in rectifying social injustices for all. Additionally, the entrepreneurs of the industrial prosperity; many of whom exploited their workers to maximise their profit margins, and others who because of strongly held beliefs looked for a more equitable way of working, framed through their own research. I will examine how those individuals built a distinctly different city – Birmingham, through their need for religious self-determination, as compared to the vast sprawling neighbour – the Black Country. So named by the black seam of coal that threaded it together, through the hard, laborious toil and the sweat of its people. I will examine the political twists and turns, which firstly transformed the parliamentary rights of the public, granting greater rights to franchise for some men and excluding that right from women altogether with the same sweep of the pen. Then the shifting nature of politics that gave way to a more Liberal and the Socialist doctrine, as governments came and went. I will analyse the many catalysts of that change, the social reformers and the various interest groups; the non-conformist churches and the Fabian Society.

Most importantly the rise of the women's trade union movement, eventually led to the establishment of the National Federation of Women Workers, who under the outstanding leadership of Mary Macarthur became enablers for much of that change. This peaceful revolution was for the poorest of poor, the hard-pressed women workers, trying to eek out a living to support flagging family incomes, at a time of inflationary rises, and exploitative middlemen. Women without rights to protection from danger, without rights to regulation, who were seen as a cheap supply of labour and of no consequence to anyone. In particular, the women chainmakers of Cradley Heath, who although possessing a skill to manufacture a much needed item, were treated as unskilled and worthless; enslaved to their forges.

I shall elaborate on their lives, how they lived and tried to maintain their families. The arduous nature of their work; combining great physical stamina and fortitude, with the long hours and ever-present dangers. Their impoverished living conditions; where children went without food or were put to bed when mother – after a ten-hour day – maintained the family laundry as best she could. The little town of Cradley Heath itself, so ingrained in the poverty of its people, who had no rest, no time for leisure, that it had become a colourless environment referred to in articles as a 'black spot'. For any soul, living their life was merely about maintaining an existence from one meal to the next; from one birth to the next; until you died.

This book is not about feminism or the Suffragettes; they were fighting a very different battle to this. Mary Macarthur was staunchly anti-feminist and aligned herself with the rights to Universal Suffrage, believing passionately that everyone deserved to be given a right to vote and that it should not be determined along lines of gender. Neither is this a book concerning trade unionism per se, I do not consider myself qualified or knowledgeable enough about a topic so vast, as to try and do it justice in this text. I am endeavouring to bring balance to a story that in some ways has become mythologised, inadvertently, due to the use of new tactics and exploitation of the media. In my opinion this has to be one of the first cases of 'spin' ever employed in the British Press. That is not to decry in anyway the excellent field of publicity that was given to a cause in much need of attention; I just wish to bring the weight of fact to bear on the media saturation that has become enmeshed in much of our common understanding of events that happened then.

In the French language the word for 'story' is 'histoire' and that is exactly what history is, it is a collection of stories told and retold, some more objectively than others. When we tell a 'story' we invariably put weight on the things that matter to us in the re-telling of that story, and that in turn, creates a slant on the emphasis of what happened and how it happened. I have written before that history is a dangerous territory for any author to explore. One has to commit to words, one's version of that 'story'. It becomes the view of that person, no matter how we try to balance it against citation, or fact, it is always 'an interpretation' of that story; my interpretation. It can create a minefield, as it can be read in many different ways, due to another person's understanding of that written word, that is why I say that my story is subjective, it is what I understand the story to be (Debney 2006, Debney 2010).

I am placing before you the facts as I read them and understand them, from a collection of sources; books written by many different types of author (academic and non-academic), from archive records (generally press cuttings), from memoirs (Rebecca's Story), from anecdote and observation. I have woven all that I can into a tapestry and have endeavoured to analyse what is there. It is important to say at this point that no event can ever be distilled into one essence, or even a simple timeline of action and event; throughout the reading of this book it should become apparent that there were a multitude of forces and triggers coalescing, that would eventually culminate in the Cradley Heath dispute. No one thing can be identified as the essence, not even a small collection of things, there were many diverse happenings which sought to converge in this one moment in history.

This story holds a personal place in my heart, as with my previous book 'The Dangerfields', I believe in order to write with passion on any topic, there must be a personal inspiration that comes first. I lived in the Black Country for six years of my life, I made a home in 'The Lye' and in Stourbridge when I trained as a glassmaker, I became attached to the people and their culture; their funny dialects and language. When I proceeded to train as a teacher in Dudley, my very first teaching practice was at Cradley Heath High School, there I learnt that the diversity from town to town, was a marked characteristic of the Black Country. There is an enormous sense of belonging, and a desire to keep alive the traditions and history that keeps this mass of people proud of where they come from and what they stand for.

Much of what was their industry has gone and been replaced by the new. The Round Oak Steel Works, became the sprawling Merry Hill Shopping

Complex; many of the world famous glassmakers, such as Stuart Crystal, are no more. Despite recession after recession, and the loss of large centres of manufacturing there is still the hope and determination of the people in a future. All is not lost, the Black Country Living Museum is doing an excellent service to the community in keeping the history and tradition ever-present for all to see. Every year in September it has become a focal point for the Regional TUC to come together to celebrate what trade unionism has achieved through the Chainmakers' Festival. This year will undoubtedly be a spectacular event to mark the 100 years since that enormous achievement came to pass at Cradley Heath. As each year turns to the next, so the Black Country will survive and reinvent itself to make an indelible mark on future histories; just as each chainmaker added her mark to the pledge to stand firm and see the strike through to the end.

Chapter 1

THE MELTING POT OF CHANGE

This story does not begin in 1910, but at a much earlier time in the political history of the UK. It is not just centred on an area of the Midlands, but is in fact the culmination of a much greater struggle that was being fought on the national political stage. When analysing any historical happening, it is all too easy to try to distil events, in an effort to reach the essence of the causes and practicalities that led to a particular moment. To my mind, this is a flawed exercise doomed to failure, as the complexities of any social society – with factions and self-interest – makes this an impossible task; rather one should try to build a canvas from all of the facts available to assemble as vivid a picture as possible to allow the reader to articulate their own conclusions.

From the outset of my research, it became clear to me that this story was not just an incident in isolation which achieved a monumental outcome, it was in fact, the culmination of a far greater tapestry of events. In this chapter, I will attempt to describe for you the context that led to the strike and the socio-political melting pot that had been boiling on the national stage for some time.

As I have already stressed, this is not a book about women's suffrage or the fight for female emancipation, but as that was one of the major issues of the time, it is as much part of this story; and the Acts of Parliament that had disenfranchised women and created the social inequalities that were evident in 1910. Further, although the complexities of the political spectrum fifty, or more years, preceding the strike may seem irrelevant, by describing them I hope that you will gain a sense of the massive social change which was precipitated by the evolving face of politics.

It would be fair to argue that the starting point of this story was the Reform Act 1832, an Act designed to increase the right to franchise; the right to vote. At this time, the country's political system was divided between two political parties, the Tories and the Whigs; the Tories were viewed as landed gentry, and the Whigs who had traditionally spoken for the common people and supported non-conformist Protestantism, yet were of the same social standing as their rivals. This is a very simple analysis, for it generalises many who did not fit into either of those definitions, and disregards the fact that because the right to vote had been restricted for so long, it was designed to serve the interests of electing those that governed, thus perpetuating the continuity of the same ruling classes.

Furthermore, there had been many politicians who had real desires to drive social change, one only has to consider William Wilberforce and the campaign for the abolition of slavery to appreciate this; these individuals can be found on both sides of the House and were not necessarily divided along party lines. However, more and more, through the earlier years of the nineteenth century, politics was factionalising and those that considered themselves to be for social reform moved firmly into the Whig camp, and those that sought to protect the self-interest of land owners and aristocracy sat firmly with the Tories.

The Representation of the People Act of 1832, set out to attempt to redress the political imbalance that had served the political elite, allowing them to have greater power in the House of Commons through weight of numbers. It sought to reduce the number of MPs that could be elected through the use of 'pocket' or 'rotten' boroughs, making way for a much fairer democratic system. At the same time, the right to franchise, the right to vote, was extended to more individuals; it only actually increased the voting population from 400,000 to 650,000. It was the wording of the Act that created the historical precedent that set the course of struggle for the next century.

The term 'male persons' was used to define those that would receive franchise, these words entered the statute books and legally barred women from having any rights to a political voice. Those that had argued for a more equitable outcome, were silenced by the advocates of the Act, on the grounds that women's interest would be best served by their husbands and men-folk. The effect of the Act was to enshrine in law women as the political underclass with no franchise rights until 1918 – and then only limited to specified few of the female population. Consequently, from 1832 onwards a movement of dissatisfied social reformers began to emerge, who felt that women had been particularly ill-served, also that the rights of franchise had to be extended to a much wider section of the male population.

Then there was the rise of the non-conformist churches and other societies that were bred in the towns and villages. The Unitarians, the Quakers, the Congregationalists, to name a few, they rose from the Evangelical Church movement, which sought to define religious practices in a more democratic fashion; adopting direct New Testament translations.

These churches were more accessible to the common people, they were viewed as less corrupt than the traditional high-church establishment. They looked to educate their congregation and be more active in their general social welfare. Some, like the Quakers called for greater biblical observance; the abstention from alcohol, the restriction on supporting political parties, or ideologies. These churches and the various philanthropic societies that formed as a consequence later in the century – like the Fabians – had a revolutionary effect on the many people in the country who had no rights to elect their own government; these bodies recognised them as people which gave them a form of empowerment.

A very present and tangible fear pervaded some quarters of the government that without real reform revolution might spring from discontent. There had been one in France, our closest neighbour, again sparked by poverty and suppression, so there were those who were active to seek compromise. As Foucault points out (1998) power is not something that comes from above, we allow others to have power over us, thus it follows, that there will inevitably come a time where if that power is too greatly abused, we will react.

Another form of revolution was taking place around the country. The invention of the steam engine by James Watt and the subsequent partnership with Matthew Boulton, was changing the face of the production of goods. Initially, driving the cotton industry in Lancashire, it then spread into every sector creating the new mass production of commodities. These inventions required two resources in large quantities; iron and coal. It was a Quaker family, the Derbys, based in Coalbrookdale, who pioneered the method of iron production in their coke-fired furnaces; the development to produce steel followed swiftly.

Soon centres of mechanised production were springing up around the UK at sites where there were ample supplies of the raw materials needed. The Midlands had been the birthplace of these innovations, by virtue of the area's enormous mineral wealth, and the region would remain the most important centre of manufacturing for the next century. As the infrastructure of canals, and subsequently, railway networks grew, so the importance of this conurbation to the national economy grew evermore significantly.

The other major resource that was required for manufacture was manpower, and with the poverty that had accompanied agriculture for centuries, many were attracted from a wide surrounding area to migrate into these new industrial centres in order to make a living. My own family made the same journey from rural Staffordshire towards Birmingham and The Black Country. The men who drove these new industries, were on the whole, individuals with the money to invest – historically the land owners and the wealthy families – this is particularly true of the Lancashire Cotton Industry. They were not philanthropic individuals, but men with a desire to accumulate even greater wealth from their newly founded enterprises, these ambitions inevitably led to greater exploitation of the underclass of workers.

In the nineteenth century, the population growth went from just over eight million at the turn of the old century, to thirty million at the turn of the next. This was an explosion on a monumental scale, a certain amount was due to migration of others to England, in particular the Irish. This was combined with a physical necessity for families to be larger, as infant mortality was high, there was a need to produce surviving children who would one day support their ageing parents. There was also a requirement for more people, to drive the ever expanding industrial efforts; more working children, meant a greater income. Not that the incomes were particularly high, for most they were well below the level of subsistence. Exploitation meant that the costs were kept down in order to keep manufacturing profits high, and workers were an expendable commodity; there were always plenty more to take their place if they died or left.

Despite a substantial rise in economic growth at 0.3% annually till 1820 in England, with the accompanying rise in the cost of living, wages were low; and for the rest of that century fell in actual terms against the rising costs. This had obvious consequences, on health and welfare, as with any population conurbation where people are concentrated into smaller, and smaller areas of living. Those who had previously worked in more rural locations, had been able to eek out a living, all be it basic, from the land. Their health suffered less and infant mortality was lower, but once there was no longer the opportunity to find food from other sources, intensive town dwellers became dependent on the food and fuel that their inadequate wages could buy them. This led to a massive rise in poverty, and all of the associated evils that accompany it such as criminal activity and malnutrition. The rise in communicable disease, cholera and typhoid, followed the intense living conditions which were being established in the rapidly expanding towns that lacked adequate water supplies and sanitation.

However, the Reform Act of 1832, did establish a new concept with the new voting profile – the middle class. These were neither landed gentry, nor poor workers, they were those of the semi-professional, professional strata; doctors, lawyers, businessmen. This new class of people were more able to self-determine their progress in life and posed a real threat to the established system. Their emergence created some discomfort, for the government were only too aware that it had been the middle class in France who had driven the revolution. These people were to be respected and placated, and were to be raised up to aspire to better things, rather than associate themselves with those of lower demeanour.

By encouraging the middle class to the possibility of social aspiration – though the fact was probably true that it was completely impossible for them to reach a more elevated station – it was thought that these bourgeoisie would disassociate themselves with the majority of the population; hence posing no threat to the established status quo. As this group aspired towards politics, they were actively encouraged to do so, obviously towards the Whigs side of the house, and in turn, they began to drive the need for social change for themselves; greater educational opportunities, better health provision and so on.

Political evolution was an inevitable consequence, there were too many well educated, like-minded, men in government to allow the present conditions to continue to flourish. There was a real desire emerging to redefine the governing authority of the land; a country that was now entering a modern age at ten times the speed it had fifty years earlier; the political spectrum had to take account of this and recognise it. There were also many debating societies and pressure groups springing up in different parts of the country, spouting new intellectual creeds of true democracy and rights, that could no longer be ignored. It was obvious to the more creative thinkers in government that things had to change and fast.

The birth of Liberalism was in fact a revolution in its own right, the newly adopted title of many Whigs, which was the party led by William Gladstone from 1867. It was in fact a coalition of a collection of diverse opinions, but it was an opposition to what had existed previously, if one of instability and vulnerability. It was the party that could represent those in the middle class, and would attract many of these business people and entrepreneurs into political life for the first time. It was from this party that most social change began to be promoted. The Liberals represented a diverse political spectrum of interests and causes; from those that believed that the strength of the empire determined the wealth of the nation, to those who posited that only by raising the lower classes out of poverty could the nation achieve real economic stability. Men like Joseph Chamberlain were drawn into the political arena, promoting the growth of entrepreneurial capitalism; and Sir Charles Dilke emphasising the need for social reform.

With such extremes of difference ever-present, it was inevitable that the party would be too factional to survive as an intact entity, and eventual questions of Irish Home Rule and Free Trade forced permanent division. Joseph Chamberlain led a Liberal Unionist split, which pushed the Liberals out of government for twenty years. However, before this they had managed to pass the third Reform Act of 1884, which increased the electorate to a total of 5,500,000.

For some in the country, the process of political change was too slow and did not represent enough of the populace. The rise of the Socialist movement spearheaded by the likes of Kier Hardie and Robert Smillie, became a beacon to many individuals who wanted to push for a new way. Many of the debating societies and interests groups found themselves drawn into the concept of socialism and all that it stood for, but it would not be till after the Great War when this new political movement would become a real force for change. Until then it had to be left to those Liberals to share their power to promote socialism; the Liberal ideals were more in accordance with the socialist philosophy than the Conservatives, to best represent these views.

On the outside of government, were the multitudinous collection of pressure groups and organisations, which were at that time acting as the catalysts for change. Groups such as the early female suffrage unions, the Fabians, the Quakers (who by their beliefs could not have political associations) and the rising Trade Unions. These and many others sought to lobby any MPs who could voice their opinions; by writing and publishing literature and holding rallies to raise public awareness and support.

All of this acceleration of change into the modern world, was accompanied by a vanguard of new technology, which would make the whole pace of life faster and more accessible. Rail networks would transform the landscape and speed up travel, carrying news of one happening hundreds of miles in a day. Much later, the invention of telegraphy and common use of the telephone, would enable information to pass quickly, which meant decision-making would become a vastly accelerated process. This in turn would make widespread communication through newspapers a common happening; everyone, everywhere would know and form opinion, on any event large or small. The age of the mass media had dawned and those with specific interests to promote their causes, or highlight their tragedies would learn to manipulate this new medium to full advantage; soon moving images would add to that drama.

Further to all this, were the cultural shifts in society, which were being precipitated by the new emerging class. The Victorian dogma of living was being shaken off; what had been considered 'right and proper' was now being questioned. Old moralities and standards of behaviour, were being overturned for the blatant hypocrisies that they had hidden from view. The middle class had created their own social codes which though emulating traditional Victorian values, were on the whole more observant towards biblical and religious doctrine; the cultural norms of this new class were exposing the excesses of those that had been the ruling classes.

That is not to say that the middle class did not wish to become part of the new consumerism that was sweeping the nation. As mass production of every conceivable manufactured item rose, so too did the demand, and this demand then generated an even greater need for the products, goods and services. The sweeping pace of technological advancement was driving the desire to be part of the new, have more, want more; all of which had to be produced, and although many things could be turned to mechanised processes, there were many more things that could not.

Products such as the chains of this book, still depended on labour intensive, manual production; machines that had been tried were ineffective in producing the rigorous quality needed. Manufacturing methods had beem outmoded in a modern age, when production could no longer keep up with demand. We must not forget that Great Britain headed an Empire, and had to provide for many other markets internationally, which put even greater demands on the workers. As these processes could not be mechanised; and thus did not appeal to the businessmen as investments for plant and machinery; they remained as cottage industries 'homework'.

There was always someone to exploit this 'homework', an overseer, a middleman (or woman), who was more than happy to make money on the backs of others. To do so, they had to keep their costs down, in order to make the contracts for the large enterprises which were their customers; in turn they kept their payments to the minimum to their suppliers. The vast supply of labour, meant there was always someone, less well off and more hungry, willing to carry out low-skilled tasks for less and less income. This exploitation began to spill over into the semi-skilled and skilled homeworking sector; the chainmakers, the shirt makers, the lace makers, and as each generation passed, so these practices would become custom.

As the collective pressures of living began to effect every area of production, so some workers began to organise. The emergence of trade unionism was a direct response by those strong enough to voice dissatisfaction, inevitably because of the inequalities of the franchise it was men that led this vanguard. They were paid considerably more than their female counterparts – though not enough to be adequately rewarded for their labours – and were generally employed in factories or an organised workforce such as miners. Their sheer weight of numbers convinced some employers to take their demands seriously, though in the earlier days many disputes were put down by some force such as the earlier chainmaking strikes.

Women were not considered to be of importance, either, by the employers, or the trade unions – many of whom held firm with the belief that women were undercutting the wages of their male counterparts. Various trade unionists of the time fought vigorously to discourage the employment of women, such as Richard Juggins and W. J. Davies (Morgan 2001) who led the earlier metal trades organisations of Birmingham and the Black Country. They were of the belief – as many were – that women working (especially married women) were an abomination. However it took others to create the discourse that if men were paid an adequate wage their wives and daughters would not have to work. This division of male workers from female was a gender-based discourse to actively exclude women, which set the longer-term precedent with (what were to become) the established engineering unions.

The social enlightenment that had dawned caused those of conscience to question these gross exploitations of the poor, to examine the causes and seek remedies. Many such as Clementina Black and Robert Sherard wrote texts upon the subject of 'sweating', as homework was now defined, and the abomination that it was in a modern society. As the century turned, more social reformers and societies began to produce texts to highlight their studies. The Fabians analysed the problem in detail through the contributions of Elizabeth Hutchins, Beatrice and Sydney Webb; later Edward Cadbury, Cecile Matheson and George Shann added their closer analysis. Edward Cadbury, in particular, went on to produce some well-timed works, where he examined the conditions of poverty and offered his own suggestions from the methods of good practice that Cadbury's as a company had promoted through their Quaker beliefs.

Emma Paterson, Clementina Black and subsequently Emilia Dilke, were the first to raise the cause of the women of the chainmaking industry; initially through a feminist discourse of the attempts by the unions to exclude women from the occupation on the basis of their gender. As their observation of these women became more informed and in-depth, they realised that this was a reductionist argument and the real causes of the exploitation that had driven such great division amongst the working class unions, was poverty. Women had to work to help their families to survive. As they became established as workers in such skilled occupations as chainmaking, they considered it a right to be able to continue; the artisanal discourse of those practising a skilled craft (Morgan 2001). However, as they were not organised (and under the present union conditions) never likely to be, they were an easy source for exploitation by those middlemen/women who viewed the women as the cheapest source of labour, enabling them to increase their own income.

The Women's Protective and Provident League (which became the Women's Trade Union League) began to draw people's attention to the various problems of sweated workers – particularly women. Many critics of these female movements tried to divide the public opinion by exposing these endeavours as feminist suffrage – still an unpalatable movement in the public consciousness. But there were others who listened and felt ashamed of the exposed ills of the industrial age.

It would not be long before all those with a vested interest in promoting the need for substantial social reform would began to unify under one banner, that chance came with the National Anti-Sweating League, which I shall discuss in greater detail in chapter 7. This movement would promote the cause through a discourse of class and remove the problem from that which had been perceived as an issue of gender. This was a dawning of social philanthropy driven by strong academic research, from those with the education and initiative to drive progressive change that could no longer be ignored.

In the next chapter, I shall isolate the area of the Black Country and Birmingham, and place the evolution of that area on the socio-political map. I shall endeavour to examine how the natural wealth of the mineral deposits drove the centring of the industrial age there, and brought with that all of the associated problems; and subsequently those with the need to resolve the social inequities that this industrial wealth caused.

Chapter 2

WHERE THERE'S MUCK, THERE'S MONEY

To most people who do not know the area of Birmingham and the Black Country, they are often confused and thought of as synonymous with one another, to those that inhabit these places this assumption could not be further from the truth. They are distinctly different, both geographically and culturally. The accents are often confused, yet there are many different dialects that make up the area called the Black Country, which gives names and words differing from any conversation that may usher forth from the Birmingham conurbation.

Comparatively speaking, the Black Country has much older origins than the relative newcomer of Birmingham, having established metal working traditions being recorded in the sixteenth century. The area that is called the Black Country, is made up of a collection of towns and villages that have merged together assuming an urban mass, and is controlled by four local authorities; Wolverhampton, Walsall, Dudley and Sandwell. Now it is contained within the county of the West Midlands, however it used to be divided between the two counties of Staffordshire and Worcestershire.

This diverse spread of towns and villages across county borders covering some 150 square miles (Barnsby 1998), assumed the general description as the Black Country, because of the extensive seam of coal that lies beneath. This seam is nine metres thick and surfaces at various places, giving rise to open cast mining, it is recognised as the thickest seam in Great Britain. The combined blackness of the coal, and the industrial trades that came with it, led to this descriptive title, which the many inhabitants are proud to assume, though their distinct local differences are of greater importance to them.

Birmingham, on the other hand, was merely a small town, that grew exponentially with the rise of the political importance that the area attracted. Birmingham is three hundred metres above sea level, sitting on the named Birmingham Plateau. In the days of the early growth of the town this rise in landfall did pose a logistical problem of bringing materials in and sending goods out. The development of the extensive canal network that now criss-crosses the city, following on shortly thereafter with the advent of the railway, enabled the town to respond to the demand for manufactured goods, first nationally and then internationally to all the far flung extents of the empire. It is said that there are more square miles of canal in Birmingham than in Venice, at the peak of use Birmingham could boast more than two hundred and fifty-seven kilometres of canal, now just under half of that is navigable.

The same metal trades established themselves there, as in the Black Country, at about the same time, and with that came the reputation for crafted engineering; especially small arms and jewellery, which developed Birmingham's importance nationally. As these trades grew, so they attracted more investment and those with the money to invest to the area; which in turn encouraged some forward thinking and intelligent men to the place that was still a town. They brought with them a political awareness and intellect, that was focused in one area and easier to disseminate through the town than in the much wider spread Black Country.

Taking the nineteenth and twentieth centuries as our focus the population of the entire Black Country, in the census of 1801 is given as 97,242, by the turn of the next century it is recorded as 671,009. Although as Barnsby 1990, is in haste to point out;

"The rate of growth varied considerably over the century, and the growth rate of individual towns varied even more."

The population of Birmingham is given as 73,670 in 1801, and by 1901 it had risen to 522,204 and by 1911 (the time of the subject of this book) it was standing at 840,202. Which is quite startling when one considers that the population is just over a million now, and the land area as given in 1887, John Bartholomew's *Gazetteer of the British Isles*, as just under eleven and a half square acres or eighteen square miles (www.visionofbritain.org.uk). The city had absorbed a number of other parishes by 1911, but had always been a very small area for such a high population. Birmingham was incorporated as a borough in 1838, but despite its very large population did not gain incorporation as a city until 1889.

It is clear from a comparison of statistics that Birmingham more so than the Black Country experienced an influx of migrant workers from the surrounding counties, whereas the area of the Black Country comprising as it does of thirty places in the census returns has pockets of substantial increase. It appears to occur at what would become the prominent places of industrial expansion such as; Tipton from 1801 to 1811 having a growth recorded of 96%, or Smethwick between 1831 and 1841 recording an increase of 88% (Barnsby 1990). It is possible to draw the conclusion that a new industry had begun and attracted many new workers quickly.

Birmingham was expanding rapidly and offering work in many of the trades associated with the massive urban expansion, such as; building and construction. From my own experience, my family who had been a family of master builders and stone masons in Gnosall in Staffordshire, came to Birmingham en-masse to find work, which of course opened up new opportunities for them. Success breeds success, as more migrated and created the need for more, so more work followed. There was plenty of work for those that were willing to apply themselves and get on with it. That was of course as long as the country was in boom times, when the country hit recession Birmingham did too, and this forced many to accept less and less money in order to stay alive (much of this book will cover the sweated trades that arose from such lean times).

When times were so difficult, men could no longer make an adequate wage to support their families, as prices were undercut time and again. This forced the wives and other women of the family out to work, at first to supplement family income, but in time to make the family income. Women were not counted as independent householders with rights, and subsequently were easily exploited by mercenary employers, who knew that they could be paid less because they were women, and because they could not be organised by trade unions.

However, when the country was at war, or our military outposts in various parts of the empire needed fresh armaments, Birmingham was the centre of that trade and thrived as a consequence. Birmingham Small Arms was a trade association of fourteen arms manufacturers, which formed in 1861, when they were called on to supply the massive contracts for the Crimean War. George Kynoch too, established his first operation at that time, manufacturing percussion caps at Witton.

As Birmingham became more noted for its finer engineering work and the mass production of machined goods, the Black Country tended to remain in the traditional crafts; Stourbridge, Dudley and Brierley Hill famed for the hand-blown glass, Dudley for the hand-beaten, hollow-ware, and Cradley for chains. More to the north and east of the region it was locks and machining in Willenhall and a smaller chain making industry in Walsall. Crafts that should have become extinct with the advent of the machine age, did not die out in the Black Country because it was for most the only income that they could get and as such they would work for a paltry sum. It was a case of these trades being kept alive by the sweaters for their own personal advantage, living off the backs of those who could do nothing else. That is not to say that Birmingham did not have more than its fair share of exploited workers, which I shall discuss more later in this chapter.

As different as these two places were in landmass and population distribution, so their political map contrasted too, because of the differences in religion and occupation. The late eighteenth century was a time of war and revolution on the international stage, the American War of Independence (1775-83), was quickly followed by the French Revolution (1789) and then war broke out with France in 1793. This created great economic instability within our own country and led to escalating food prices. It was a time of middle and working class rebellion against the ruling elite, something that had been emerging for most of that century in the rest of the UK too, as Barnsby 1993, notes:

"From 1700 to 1815 the typical form of working class protest was the riot. At a time when a very large proportion of wages was spent on food and prices varied enormously due to bad harvest and bad communications the food riot by a 'mob' was a very effective form of protest."

The right to vote had been historically restricted in order to perpetuate the status quo of those who were the landed gentry being the governing class, as such there were MPs for the counties, but none representing the very large towns that were developing. The Black Country had no MPs which meant not only were the working class not represented, but neither were middle class (Barnsby 1993). The town of Birmingham was represented by the two MPs for Warwickshire. More and more, people began to show their dissatisfaction for the system through protest, as every economic depression arose, so did the working class and middle class anger, only disrupted in times of war.

Birmingham was unincorporated, and as such had attracted many of those from other religious determinations that had found themselves discriminated against by the traditional dogma of Anglicanism, both church and state had sought various sanctions against practicing non-conformists, that had forced them to seek sanctuary where the state had little interference. From that point of view, Birmingham had attracted many illuminated individuals from a more freethinking and radical determination. Families such as the Cadburys, the Kendricks, the Martineaus, et al (Ward 2005), would find themselves settled and established there as those of greatest influence. The inventors Boulton and Watt who formed the thinking elite, would form the Lunar Society, which although short-lived would contribute towards the body of knowledge. Boulton would push for the establishment of the Birmingham Assay Office eventually founded in 1773 (Ward 2005), which placed Birmingham centrally on the map of fine metal production, second to none outside the capital.

This core of non-conformity would affect the way in which the two places Birmingham and the Black Country, would progress with the onset of the industrial revolution, and how they would agitate for political change. Whereas the Black Country would eventually show a preference to radical secularism that would mobilise the working classes – in contrast to the unincorporated neighbour – the Black Country was doomed to live in the shadow of the cheeky-young-upstart town. For as Birmingham attracted all of the enlightened into a small concentrated area, so it was able to capitalise on the entrepreneurial skills of those who were used to having to challenge the status quo daily, just to be allowed to live a normal life.

As the eighteenth century turned, Britain found herself once again caught in the grip of conflict of the Napoleonic wars. For the entire area which was built on the skills of metal working, war was always a time of plenty, particularly for Birmingham which although still manufacturing on a small scale, was building an excellent reputation for the production of weaponry and armaments. Though the town itself was slow to embrace the very invention that was created there, which was bringing the north of England greater prosperity – the Boulton and Watt steam engine. But as Birmingham became mechanised so the Black Country remained entrenched in the workshop and mining culture.

The first half of the nineteenth century was dominated by three significant periods of economic depression, all three would have a great impact on all of the towns of the Black Country and Birmingham, and give rise to organised political agitation which would impact on national government. The first ran immediately after the Napoleonic wars 1815 to 1823, then the next was three years later 1826 to 1833, and the last one ran from 1839 to 1843 (Barnsby 1998). After each, as Barnsby 1989 notes, there was an 'upsurge in working class activity'. But this was a more muted and organised reaction (and agitation) to that which had previously transpired with their dissatisfaction, as Barnsby records 1989:

"In came new, modern institutions – working class newspapers, trade unions co-operative organizations, Socialist policies and working class political parties."

The middle classes led the vanguard, those with a specific interest to do so, the entrepreneurs particularly in Birmingham, who found themselves without a voice, other than through intensive parliamentary lobbying. The city was over 100,000 strong and could neither raise its own police force or courts of law, a situation that could not continue; never mind the needs of public services, such as adequate street lighting and housing.

The radical free press of William Cobbet and others had planted the seeds of insurrection and peaceful protest, a 'Union' was founded in Birmingham, seeking universal suffrage and annual parliaments (Ward 2005). In the Black Country similar unions were formed and the working classes and the middle classes moved as one to fight the inequalities. This was part of the national 'Chartists' movement that continued on into the middle of the century pushing for political reform, for many at much personal cost, imprisonment, even loss of life in the case of the Peterloo Massacre 1819.

The Birmingham Political Union attracted a very charismatic leader, a banker from Halesowen called Thomas Attwood. Unlike his more radical contemporaries, such as Fergus O'Connor, Attwood always muted his language when pressing for change while in obedience to the law. Again and again, the influence of the BPU brought applied pressure onto the successively, besieged governments of this explosive time. At one point in 1832 it is recorded that Attwood would only have had to have given his word, to call all to arms, and there would have been mass-insurrection which would have probably overthrown the government (Ward 2005). It certainly had the desired effect of forcing the Great Reform Act through, but at a cost to the radical movement as a whole, for through the extension of the franchise to middle class, the working class were divided and resentful. Particularly in the Black Country, where the links of individual churches did not keep those that served in line with their masters. The Black Country, being mainly Anglican, resented the churches suppression as much as that of their factory owners and bosses, this led to a rise of radicalism in opposition to the Chartists – who were viewed as a dying organisation – the Secularists.

Ultimately, both these factions led to culture amongst the working class of the need to organise into a unified body in order to maintain strength. The working man's trade union had been outlawed, but became commonplace nationally, though not as strong as might have been assumed in the industrialised Midlands. With all that had gone before, the threat of real uprising and with the beginning of the changes in government, by the 1850's trade unionism was beginning to have clout in some quarters. Though women would remain on the periphery for some time to come, for the damage caused by the Great Reform Act of 1832 would have repercussions far beyond.

As women were excluded from franchise, so they were deemed as 'less than' and in the case of the working classes, much less than. A working man struggling to make an income to support his family, was often undercut by a woman working for less (which they would do, for that was what was expected of them). Consequently, the unions resented the intrusion of women on men's jobs and men's incomes and excluded them from the unions. It followed that as the women could not be organised, so it lay them open to exploitation by the sweater. Both Birmingham and the Black Country had many examples of this; from chains to hollowware, card board box manufacture, to button carders, etc, to name a few.

Thus, when the next great political star rose in the firmament of Birmingham, it was in a very divided society, of those who had rights to vote and those who had nothing (not even a living wage), he sought to make changes to the lives of those many disadvantaged. These changes that would make difference for the vast majority who lived there, but it would cast a severe contrast against the impoverished state of the bigger neighbour. Joseph Chamberlain was an enigma, and to Birmingham probably their greatest adopted son, he certainly rose to greater political heights than Attwood, but never succeeded to the position of the highest seat in the land – as his youngest son Neville would one day aspire. It was assumed by many that this political aspiration was in no doubt; but rather he became master of his own downfall, if not a casualty of the Great Depression; however, he was never to fall entirely from grace, not for the good folk of Birmingham. His success was due to a combination of birth and being in the right place at the right time.

Chamberlain's political ascendency began to manifest itself, as the political map of Birmingham and the Black Country emerged from the darkness. Barnsby (1998) elaborates on the poor position of the electorate for Birmingham and the Black Country pre-1832, and how the Reform Act brought power finally to the conurbations with Birmingham and Wolverhampton gaining two seats each, and Walsall and Dudley one seat each. This group of six seats, then tended to fall into Liberal hands with frequency, simply because the Liberals were the best representatives of the middle class factory owners (akin to Chamberlain), who were the voting populace in the newly extended franchise; only Dudley would be returned as Tory on occasion, due to the historical royalist connections.

The Liberals sought to retain control nationally, and had no desire to extend the franchise unduly, however, as Barnsby (1998) quotes they were caught out by the Conservatives when Disraeli 'stole their clothes', as they sought to manage 'fancy Franchises' and passed the second Reform Act in

1867. This effectively gave the franchise to most male householders in towns; it increased the voting population of Birmingham by 150 percent. Which gave a greater mandate to any Liberal standing in that area, and real strength to the local party in general.

The more enlightened Liberals, such as Chamberlain, realised that because of this extension to franchise, concessions and promises would now have to be given to this new voting public in order to secure their loyalty. He and others like him, got himself a reputation as a Radical Liberal, for his policy of self-taxation of the middle class in order to fund reforms and improvements.

Chamberlain had been born in London to Joseph Chamberlain senior, a shoemaker. His father had acquired shares in his brother-in-law's business interests in Birmingham, manufacturing screws; Joseph junior was sent to learn the business. This he did with great aplomb, possessing a head for thorough analysis and an eye for detail. With his business acumen to the fore, he created a thriving enterprise, so much so, that when the business was eventually sold in 1874, he was able to turn his full attention to his developing political career with the £120,000 fortune he had amassed from the sale. He had also made a dynastic marriage to Harriet Kenrick in 1861, another influential family of the city, which produced his son Austen. However, in 1863 Harriet had died in childbirth, so Joseph married her cousin Florence, this match produced Neville, but tragically Florence died in 1875. Leaving Joseph under forty with six children to care for, and Mayor of the city since 1873 (Ward 2005).

His answer to his misfortune, was to throw himself headlong into his efforts to modernise the decaying Victorian city and at the same time to radicalise the Liberal movement, which he viewed as tired and moribund. He was fortunate, as the recent government legislation that had been passed assisted Chamberlain in his desire to place his name firmly on the political map. He was able to make sweeping changes in housing and education, but his most notable achievements were the municipalisation of the gas and water supplies; much of the negotiations he carried out personally to ensure success (Ward 2005).

His charisma and business skills dominated Birmingham and the local party. His grip was absolute, on what was dubbed the Liberal Caucus and as Birmingham followed with him so did the Black Country, although his radical changes, which brought him the title 'the Great Municipaliser', did little to impact on the vast majority of working class lives there and thereabouts. It was a strange time, for as he was transforming the decay of

Birmingham, into the most modern city in the world, the country as a whole was entering a deep cutting recession. But as was always the way during those times of severe downswing, as an area of great industrialisation the Midlands was always capable of seeking markets elsewhere and more often than not, offsetting some of the worst effects.

Chamberlain had his ambitious eyes set on much greater things, and by the time he had resigned as Mayor in 1876, he was returned as MP unopposed and he headed for London. There he was to be confronted with the 'old boys network', which would only ever partially accept him. For the remainder of his political career – despite being in the Cabinet for a time and the leader of the break away Liberal Unionists, he was a man of obvious political strength – he would be derided for his accent and his middle class origins; factory owners, were not considered to be acceptable to those of consequence.

Not to be put off by this, Chamberlain befriended another of importance in this book – Sir Charles Dilke. They became allies in their mutual need, Chamberlain for the necessary introductions and acceptance in society, and Dilke for a strong ally of power in government. For indeed they were a force to be reckoned with that Gladstone found impossible to ignore, so in a divisive act, he offered them one Cabinet post between them, Board of Trade. Chamberlain assumed the role, while Dilke eventually accepted a lesser role in the Foreign Office.

This Cabinet post was not to be the most successful for Joseph for several reasons. What had worked at a city level, could not be transposed with ease to the national stage. He found the workings of the various government departments slow and cumbersome, he probably missed much of the hands-on control he was able to apply in Birmingham. At the same time, he was at odds with Gladstone first as a radical, who the PM had viewed as too radical, and then as the Great Depression took hold, Chamberlain found himself leaning towards imperialist strength as the economic salvation of the country. His final salvo against his former leader was a resignation from high office, and the formation of the Liberal Unionists in protest against what he viewed as concessionary policy on Irish Home Rule.

As Chamberlain made his break from the national party heading his Liberal Unionist (who formed a pact with the Conservatives), so the Birmingham Caucus and the Black Country went with him. This forced those with voting rights into a dilemma, of whom to vote for? Did they vote for the Conservative/Liberal Unionist Alliance, which did not serve the interests of the common working man? Or did they vote for an extremely weakened Liberal Party, whom Chamberlain had effectively cast from office for twenty years? Or did they now seek the socialist movement who were beginning to grow both in different strands and strength?

With the political vacuum that was left by Joseph Chamberlain's swing to the right and the Black Country's pre-disposition to radicalism, combined with the rise in the working man's right to franchise; it was inevitable that socialism would begin its ascendancy in that area with force. However, this was not enough to make a difference by the time of the Cradley Heath dispute. Joseph Chamberlain was a strong influence to the area, and as he moved allegiances so the voting population followed; returning some wards as Conservative, effectively splitting the vote between the Liberals Unionists and the Conservatives.

As Barnsby (1998) records the working man was left with a choice of three directions; seeking a liberal/labour partnership under the old Gladstonian Liberalism, following the Chamberlain course of Liberal Unionism or form a separate party that was more representative of the working class? However, the formation of the Labour Representation Committee in 1900 coincided with the Boer War, which Chamberlain had interests in, followed closely by the guerrilla war in South Africa, which led to national 'jingoism' and imperialism, causing a significant falling away of socialist aspirations. It was not until the 1906 election when the first Labour MP was returned in Wolverhampton, one of the 29 returned across the country at that election.

However, four years later, the year of the strike, the economic picture was grim and many had become disenchanted with the Liberal Labour experiment. As Barnsby (1998) notes things had turned full circle that year:

"The only other general elections before 1914 were two in the same year of 1910. In the years since 1906 the political scene had again changed drastically. Voters, not at least in the Black Country where the basic industries had been destroyed, were still being seduced by the Protectionism of the Tories led as it was until 1906 by Joseph Chamberlain. When a stroke ended the career of the great radical renegade Lloyd George (the de facto leader of the Liberals) was laying the first foundations of the Welfare State with his reforms at this time and in 1910 was concerned to raise the money for both Old Age Pensions and more battleships by taxing the rich."

But locally, the picture was bleak, no Labour MPs were returned in either election; leaving the political landscape of Birmingham and the Black Country to a Conservative swing with a few Liberal MPs to be found in the Black Country.

Chapter 3

A WOMAN'S WORK?

'Oh but for one short hour
A respite however brief!
No blessed leisure for Love or Hope,
But only time for Grief!
A little weeping would ease my heart,
But in their briny bed
My tears must stop, for every drop
Hinders needle and thread!'

With fingers weary and worn,
With eyelids heavy and red
A woman sat in unwomanly rags,
Plying her needle and thread –
Stitch! stitch! stitch!
In poverty, hunger, and dirt,
And still with a voice of dolorous pitch –
Would that its tone could reach the Rich! –
She sang this 'Song of the Shirt'

(last two verses of 'The Song of the Shirt' – Thomas Hood)

There is no doubt that women were always in a supplemental role of employment prior to the nineteenth century and the advent of the industrial revolution, because of their traditionally accepted role in society. A woman's position had been very much the homemaker; she married, had the children and supplemented the family income doing whatever she could, while her husband worked to provide the main share of the income. This was a biological precedent, as any woman would agree with even now in this day and age of women trying to combine their nurturing duties with a career. It was not an anti-feminist approach, it was just what happened. There was much to do in the times before any mechanical contraption would aid housework.

There was a fire to be kept for warmth and food, meals to be cooked, generally bread to be made, children to be reared, clothed, taught. Sometimes, more often than not, an older generation of the family needed care; though not many lived to great or infirm ages. The washing and drying of clothes, was a time consuming and labour intensive job that required two days or more. A day was easily consumed in the normal household tasks, there was a little time for leisure and of course the necessity for religious observance. This was the pattern of settled existence that was known to the majority of families the length and breadth of the British Isles; a land-based agrarian economy. A small place to live, usually with access to a small portion of land for basic subsidence; the men working out as tenants to other land owners and farmers.

That is not to say that there was not a form of rural poverty, because poverty had always existed; either through misfortune, being left fending for yourself as an elderly or infirm person, or as a young orphan, or, a falling into poverty through indolence or intemperance, or trauma – in the case of many returning soldiers from various conflicts. This poverty, if not viewed by others around as the fault of the poor person through their actions, could be absorbed into a community and care given, friend helping friend, neighbour helping neighbour.

Two things caused an enormous change in people lives, particularly women, firstly the advent of mechanisation and secondly disenfranchisement. The rise in mechanisation was the first major impact on the home-based domestic economy (Hutchins 1915). Women had generally used their spare time in home-based activities to make extra money; through spinning and weaving. These were time consuming occupations that made a few extra pennies for the maker, it was also the only way to manufacture cloth and society was dependent upon the domestic spinners and weavers. With the invention of James Hargreaves' 'Spinning Jenny', Richard Arkwright's carding machine and Edmund Cartwright's mechanised loom all in the eighteenth century, the cottage industries were decimated overnight. Incomes were suddenly halved as the women were effectively forced out of their homes to seek other work. Men too, found themselves forced off the land to seek work elsewhere as the new mechanised farming methods made whole communities of rural workers redundant overnight. Only those with a traditional skill, which could not be mechanised – an artisanal skill – could exist for a while longer in the rural outskirts of the new factory conurbations. My family's skills as master builders and stone masons, meant that they were not dependent on the land but on others around them for work. Consequently, when the majority of their communities moved towards the towns, they followed them for work.

There is no doubt that from the moment that James Mill planted the seeds of thought in the minds of others, that 'fathers and husbands would protect' the interest of women in the right to franchise, that the fate of women as the underclass would be sealed for the next century. When Henry Hunt tried to modify this position during the parliamentary debate that introduced the 1832 Reform Bill, he was fighting a losing battle with his colleagues who had decided to enshrine in law the words 'male persons' from that moment it was the point of no return (Smith 2007). Women would be demoted by an Act of Parliament to 'less than' in every situation, to the extent that eventually it was just an accepted position, even to the women themselves.

As the urban centres expanded, and more and more people were thrust into the rapidly rising rural poverty, they migrated in ever greater numbers towards these new factory areas seeking work. This is a time before factory regulation and concerns about welfare; to the average northern mill owner human life was cheap, it was ten-a-penny. These new machines were never tested to see if they were safe, only the countless accidents and deaths revealed the true extent of the dangers that lay in these dark and dingy caverns. The noise was deafening, the work long and tiring, leading to even greater risk. For the first time women had to work away from their homes and a full day; firstly because the only income that they could get was low, as was their husbands, but it was much needed to support the shortfall in family income. The added effect of moving was that everything was costing more; food had to be bought it could no longer be grown, housing costs and rents were high, and became even more densely packed and insanitary, the cost of living was rising due to economic recession year on year. A woman working became an economic necessity not a supplemental income (Hutchins 1915). However, the more, and more women that arrived to the urban centres, the more demand for work that there was; too many women chasing too little work; employers were able to pay less and less, until a full day's work was done for a pittance.

The family began to suffer, mothers could no longer be the nurturer and the carer; they were forced to do a full day's work, often leaving elderly relatives to care for children. Basic needs for survival surpassed the desire to provide clothing and time for washing; the attributes of poverty grew as less could be done to care. Soon, women were forced out of many of the mechanised roles, as men saw their own incomes halved and halved again, by the expanding industrialisation. They had rights to franchise, they had rights under law, they could organise; they saw themselves as the breadwinners and providers, if there was a wage to be earned it was theirs by rights, they had families to support and they demanded the rights to employment with greater income; the domain of the machines became theirs, a woman's role was purely supplemental once again.

As this situation became entrenched, so women accepted this status quo, they deferred to their husbands, their community and societal expectations of them. Mallon's introduction to Hutchins (1915) shares this view that tradition and mechanisation combined to reduce a woman's position:

"The position of the industrial woman in modern times is closely related, one way or another to the industrial revolution, but the relation cannot be stated in any short or easy formula. The reaction of modern methods on woman's labour is highly complex and assumes many forms. The pressure on a woman worker which causes her to be employed for long hours, on low wages, in bad conditions, and with extreme insecurity of employment, is frequently supposed to be due to the development of industry on a larger scale. It is, in my view, due rather to the survival of social conditions of the past in an age when enormous increase in productive power has transformed the conditions of production."

This demotion of women's labour forced them to take whatever they could get, and as they were excluded from the heavier industrial processes, they were once again thrust into the domestic sphere of homeworking in much worse conditions than had ever existed before; performing functional tasks of assemblage of the mass produced objects which were now being produced from all areas of the new manufacturing processes; button-card workers, hook and eye carders etc. Or they were subjected to the monotonous, repetitive machining tasks that the men would not do; stamping and pressing, or applying finishes; burnishing and lacquering. All of these processes required little or no skill; the skilled work was the domain of fathers and husbands, and accepted as such.

As wages became even lower, inflationary costs spiralled and businessmen sought to protect their profits, so the women's work suffered further demotion. Soon to make an adequate income many had to use their children to make up the shortfall of their incomes; while factory owners exploited the children also for an even cheaper source of labour (Hutchins 1915). This was not just isolated to the towns and urbanised areas, one of the greatest requirements of the new industrial processes was coal, and long before deep mining became the norm, coke and breeze were taken from the surface mines (many which were evident in the Black Country) or from the pit brow. Women were commonly employed in this capacity to work as miners, certainly at the pit brow, and as we know now many women and children were exploited for cheap labour in the early shaft mining (John 1980).

Much of this exploitation of women and children went unregulated for much of the nineteenth century. Many commissions and groups raised the issues and demanded change and when it did come it could only be regulated and enforced in the factories. Much of the problem, which had been exacerbated through underpayment leading to poverty, merely became a fact of life, at home, out of sight of inspectors and regulators. Necessity, drove the need to exploit any extra pair of hands in order to make enough to eat.

According to Burnett (1974) the Census of 1815, put the figure of women over the age of 10 in employment at 2.8 million out of a population of 10.1 million. It is fair to conclude as many would not have been accurately recorded, that this figure could have been far larger. This Census is further complicated by the return on married women in employment at that time which is given as 2,630,000 who were given as no specific occupation, only 605,000 specifying one, out of a total population of married women given as 3,462,000. However, as Burnett notes most married women would probably only return 'themselves as employed if they engaged in whole-time work.'

There was a societal taboo growing at this time, that married women should definitely not work as they were taking away the chance of an income from a working man supporting a family. The fact that many did in a domestic homeworking situation was tolerated, as these were the jobs that men would not do anyway, being so underpaid. This taboo became one that framed a community; each woman deferred to common agreement, that a married woman should not take a job that deprived a family of a livelihood. This situation suited the employers, who were then at liberty to employ skilled male workers for all of the heavier mechanised tasks, which of course was at a cost, this cost could be offset by employing cheap, young, unmarried, female labour to fill in the low skilled and unskilled tasks. Generally, these girls were only expected to work for a short time, before joining the ranks of married women and leaving the factories.

Once in the outworking sector these young married women became the army of exploited female workers, glad of anything that they could get, open to the abuses of the sweater. Very few older women would be found in factory working, even if they were widowed as they were considered more expensive, they too became victims of the exploitative homeworking system. The sweated work principle became established very quickly as demand from consumers grew evermore, any process that was too expensive to mechanise was outsourced by factories to anyone who could offer to deliver the items at a decreased price to the previous supplier.

As a result the areas of Birmingham and the Black Country became centres of the over-exploitative working practices; as London had with the large manufacturing industry which had become established in the nation's capital. By the very fact that Birmingham had attracted larger quantity of entrepreneurial and enterprising families because of unincorporated status, it had a greater concentration of sweated occupations. The Black Country, on the other hand, was poorer economically because of the lack of political representation nationally, so poverty drove the inhabitants of the many towns and villages therein to seek work at whatever price. Here, it was not just the women who were reduced to the lowest paid sectors as poverty was so acute, men were often to be found in the same occupations. Black (1907) records:

"Although the cases quoted hitherto are those of women, and although the very worst instances of underpayment invariably occur among women, it must not be supposed that all homeworkers are women. In the nail and chainmaking districts many men as well as women work at the forges in their own backyards;"

This working for less and less became a perpetual struggle, which led to apathy and acceptance; there was no fight to change this situation, most thought it could not be changed. Black (1907) noted that the 'diminution' of wages drove them to exploit their children and when pressed further through 'slack time':

"...to the acceptance of yet lower pay for the sake of securing work."

This drift of many into acute poverty due to industrialisation became a feature of studies carried out by many in the late Victorian early Edwardian period; particularly those who had observed a different way of treating a workforce. Charles Booth, Seebohm Rowntree and Edward Cadbury et al. made significant contributions into the causes and effects of poverty. The studies that probably concern this story more so than the others are those conducted by Cadbury, as they tended to be located geographically and temporally to the chainmakers; indeed the chainmakers as a group formed part of the studies conducted by Cadbury.

The two texts that were published by Cadbury with others in 1907 are, 'Sweating' which he co-wrote with George Shann and 'Women's Work and

Wages: a phase of life in an industrial city', which was co-written with Cecile Matheson and George Shann. In both studies, the authors carried out comprehensive surveys of Birmingham and the Black Country examining the causes of the sweated industries, and the reasons many gave for working in such a way. Both books paint a bleak picture of people who had been defeated by life and had had to accept whatever they could get to keep food on the table. They questioned individuals and drew conclusions based on interviews, the techniques may seem primitive by the research methods of today but the analysis is comprehensive.

In 'Women's work and wages' they questioned a broad group of homeworkers (mainly women) as to why they worked at home rather than the factories (Cadbury et al 1907):

"Nearly all the home-workers who answered the question as to why they worked gave one of three reasons. The most frequent was that a husband's wage was either too small or too irregular to keep the home. Fifty two per cent. gave this answer in many varying forms, of which a frequent one was, 'Its all very well at first, but what are you to do when you've three or four children like little steps around you?' Others had worked all their lives; if the husband is a labourer earning at best 18s per week and liable to many weeks without work, no other course seems possible."

When they questioned women about their low wages in comparison to men for the text 'Sweating', the responses given proved the case that women had accepted their situation utterly (Cadbury and Shann 1907):

"When the question is put to them no one seems to be able to give any other reason why women's wages are at this particular level. The women themselves are apathetic and take their conditions of work and wages for granted. They never think about the matter, but accept the position with a kind of fatalism... When a woman replaces a man she is quite content to receive half or a third of what he got for the work and seems surprised when anyone suggests that it might be otherwise.

In the same chapter, the authors went on to identify three specified reasons why they considered a woman would accept a lower standard of wages, (Cadbury and Shann 1907):

"(a) Because her past training, or want of training, has not contributed to develop independence, but has rather been the reverse;

(b) Because she is subsidised by family or husband, this subsidising being itself at once a cause and effect of low wages; and

(c) Because women lack power of self-protection due to their failure to combine, which failure itself is due to cause (a) mentioned above, and to the fact that few women expect to be life-workers, practically all looking forward to marriage as an escape from employment."

The authors had correctly assessed the problem, the root causes of which through greater analysis, ran much deeper. Indeed, a woman had been made into a totally dependent creature (I struggle to use the word individual – for that she was not). She neither had rights or access to rights, this situation had been laid in law, but was carried down to the micro level of community and then family. Of course, she saw marriage as the only way out, of what had become for many, a monotonous, soul-destroying existence, whether in a factory or in the outwork situation. The prospect of marriage was the only hint of a shift in that dependence from parents to husband, but it offered some small hope of difference.

In their final analysis they blame the woman's previous experience for her lack of ability to 'combine'; whether that be part of a group; or organised in a union. To some extent what they write is true, experience had not taught them to, but neither did their men folk want them to, this I shall discuss in more detail shortly and most obviously many of the occupations that they could do (unless they were in a factory) were isolated (Black 1907); an isolation used to even greater advantage by the sweater. Working women were kept as a separate entity, set apart in most cases from the men, they were considered to be merely supplemental in all aspects of work life; yet the tasks they carried out were often through the longest days, with a vast output expected.

Men had protected the skilled occupation against, what they perceived as an invasion of women taking their work. The work order became demarked; skilled trades became the male domain, because justifiably they could claim the position as breadwinner for a family. As men became more dissatisfied with their working conditions they began to organise in ever greater numbers into the trade union organisations. These unions offered them protection from exploitative employers and as these unions grew in strength, they put their members into positions where they could bargain for improvements to their wages; against a loss of productivity to the employer – more often than not by the use of the strike.

Even the employers very often sort to reinforce this position of male-only unions for they knew that once women were organised into unions, this would grant them a status. If they had status then that would mean they would be open to greater regulation; ipso facto, making them more expensive to employ, cutting into profits. Through, Cadbury et al (1907) this issue of the regulation is discussed in the terms of a Commission that had been formed in 1876 to debate this subject, the authors have referenced it by quoting the case of two men of influence from Birmingham:

"Thus the Commission of 1876 had no excuse if they failed to see both sides of the question. 'Mr Joseph Chamberlain and Mr Arthur Chamberlain both Birmingham manufacturers in a large way of business, gave evidence, the one in favour of, the other against, the regulation of women's labour by law, the one demonstrating that the economic position of women was thereby improved and the demand for their labour increased; the other that their wages had risen little if at all, and that 'if there was no restrictions women now getting their 8s. or 9s would get 30s.'"

A complete nonsense for without regulation – whichever Chamberlain had suggested that line of argument – he was at liberty to pay as little as he desired.

When it came to union organisation not all industries were quite so successfully organised and had to have many attempts before the grip of the employers was released enough to enable any improvements – the male chainmakers of the Black Country being a prime example. Before many became factory workers, they had been the domestic outworkers, or working for exploitative employers in small forges. On a number of occasions the employers subjected them to 'lock-outs' when they tried to organise for better wages. It was only as the unions began to exert more power, and come under larger umbrella organisations that these smaller unions effected any difference. In the case of the chainmakers it was the combined efforts of their union with the muscle of the Walsall Trades Council, and the Nut and Bolt Workers Union under the leadership of Richard Juggins that made their employers listen.

Juggins made a very influential argument to many men in the metal trades, that women were taking away their livelihoods for working on lower and lower rates (Barnsby 1998, Morgan 2001). This had several effects on the male working population. Firstly, they tended to grow closer to their unions for strength in numbers, secondly, they made it clear that women were not to be brought into the unions – as that would grant women skilled status, they could demand skilled rates, further depriving men of their rightful income. Thirdly, they actively pursued their unions to exclude women from their trades. This last action had a reverse side, for many of these men depended on their wives and daughters incomes to supplement theirs. So it was more a case of excluding all women, except their own relatives.

This left the women unprotected from the worst excesses of unsavoury employers; not that they had any rights under law in the first place, or indeed valued themselves as individual workers worthy of protection. As the demand for chains grew even bigger and the need for much larger size chains for large ships was ordered, so men moved into the factory work environment leaving the small domestic forges to be filled by more women. Of course, as hand-hammered workers themselves, men had always considered themselves to be skilled, however, as women took over the domestic manufacture a diminution of the trade ensued, and women were viewed as doing less skilled work; so no need to organise them in to skilled workers in to the male unions.

There were some attempts at trying to organise women into trade unions during this period but generally as Thom (1998) alludes to, these infant organisations often confused organising women with female suffrage and:

"...were shaped more by the interests of social reformers than by the demands of the working women themselves."

One such attempt to protect the rights of women chainmakers of Cradley Heath at this time, fell far short of its aims. Emma Paterson of the WPPL viewed much of the regulation imposed on women because of Juggin's suggestions, as being deliberately detrimental to the employment of women. She was correct in her assumptions, but was portrayed as an interfering middle class woman, who did not know what she was talking about. Fortunately, a few years later Clementina Black and Lady Emilia Dilke were able to commence the organisation of women and by 1896, had managed to organise 400 of them, and combined with Thomas Sitch organising the male union, began to make a slight impact. However, a collapse in the trade, following another economic downturn caused membership to fall off.

A perennial problem for women on low income had always been, the decision whether to pay union dues or put bread on the table (Cadbury and Shann 1907). That was much the way it went until, Mary Macarthur was able to push the recruitment up with the concerted efforts of Julia Varley and Thomas Sitch a few years later. Even then, it had been an uphill struggle to convince women that they had a right to be organised, a right to protection; better wages and working conditions. Much of the work that the NFWW, the WTUL and the WU would do up to and beyond WW1, would be the hard job of trying to get women to organise. Though as dispute after dispute was settled, and more women protected, there is no doubt that the task became a much easier one.

Women were at the bottom of the pile in society, they were the 'unclean' having no caste or rights. This exposed them to the indignities of having to find whatever they could do to supplement their husbands or families income. Much of this additional work was tolerated, as long as it did not come into competition with the male bread-winning capacity. Unfortunately, as industrialisation took hold so the grip of the sweater on the domestic worker increased as the exploitative employers demanded more for less money. Every task became a greater struggle to make the same income, forcing many in the vicious cycle of poverty being unable to break free, because they were so near starvation and worked too hard. Consistent generational pressure, and loss of self-belief, in most of these women led to a sense of apathy and worthlessness and an inability to want to get up and fight.

Additionally, the male trade unions had stigmatised them further, blaming them for the loss of income of their members. Only with the advent of female trade unions that sought to organise for the needs of the worker, and not for the needs of social philanthropy was progress towards regulating women's working conditions and wages made.

Chapter 4

IN CHAINS

"To the on-looker they seem to have no time for thought. The left hand plies the great bellows – one, two, three. The fire glows at the first stroke. The worker's other hand turns the long iron rod, one end of which in the flame is already red. In a moment it is on the anvil, the glowing end shaped with quick hammered strokes into an unclosed link. The shaped section is then notched and broken off, while the rod goes again into the fire. The incomplete link is fixed to links already made and returns to the fire also. When it is red it comes again to the anvil and is welded, beaten this time with ringing full-blooded blows. And so nicely dove-tailed are these operations of shaping, notching, and wielding, and blowing the bellows that the worker never rests. She sweats. Her hair falls over her face. She talks to a neighbour, even attempts consolation to her querulous offspring, while the bellows are driven and a myriad of sparks are blown into her toil-worn face.

Such activity is of the very nature of chain-making. Either you work thus or you do not work at all. Even working in this incessant way how slowly the chain grows! A yard of chain may be made in an hour, of the commoner kinds even two yards or more, but to the on-looker, noting anxiously the exertions of the worker, this hour seems unending. It will have brought the operative perhaps a penny; in fewer cases a penny halfpenny. If she be gifted, indeed."

Slaves to the Forge – M. Macarthur (1910)

The first people who chose to make chains – or nails, as nailmaking pre-dates chainmaking – had to do it to make a living. That is not to assume that it was comfortable, it was probably just above subsistence. As a consequence of the overly high demand for the products, the industries attracted others who realised that they could make money from the relentless toil of those who made the products, this band of middlemen and women, were called the 'foggers.'

The Midlands had long been the place for manufacture of the 'nayle' and the production had taken place right across the region, but as Owen, 1989, explains:

"As the iron industry migrated westwards seeking wood for smelting, so the nail trade became more concentrated in the Dudley ridge. This was due to the accessibility of the River Stour and the River Severn on which the iron and pig – iron was imported from elsewhere."

As such, The Black Country, made up of its many sprawling outlying villages assumed the role of the centre of nails and chains. At the nail manufacture peak in the 1830's, it was recorded that some 50,000 were working in the production of nails (Owen, 1989). It is then that the exploitation by the 'foggers' had taken hold. Nail and chain production was a skilled enterprise, but as the largest items became centralised in factories controlled by owners, the smaller (general items) were farmed out to small back street forges.

These outhouses, often were what they were, forges behind the house, or as the industry became more exploitative, there could be a run of these in a street owned by the fogger and rented out. As the nailmaking trade began to decline, the chainmaking trade assumed greater importance and took over these existing premises. By 1883, according to Owen (1989) 'The Daily News' was recording twelve thousand nail and chain shops being operated by twenty thousand people, mainly women and children, sixteen thousand or so. Why so many women? The answer was a simple one, men did not want to work for such low rates. Most of the men had been organised into larger factories, where they were able to fight for better pay as a group from a factory owner, as the skilled workforce they received these meagre increases, for the employer knew that vast majority of his income was from the outsourced-female worker existing on much lower rates.

Times were hard, at first it would have been the women who had been taught by their fathers and brothers in the outhouses, and put to work by their male siblings as a way to supplement their family's income. Then as each subsequent generation passed, mothers would teach daughters, and pass the skills on. For some women it was their only income, as they were widows, or single. Some were supporting families only on their income as their husbands believed that it was their right to keep their wages to themselves.

In the beginning chainmaking did receive recognition for the skill required, that was probably a throw-back to when it had been mainly men employed in the small forges. But as the industry became more feminised, and as the iron-rod of the foggers assumed control, and each little forge became swallowed into supplying chain to the factories; so the status of skill became lessened.

It still took the same amount of hard work and ability to 'shut' the chain, but as is true with many industries where the wages are steadily reduced it became deskilled in perception, because no one believed that there could be any skill in a process where someone earned so little for their labours. However, it had been the case that these skills were considered to be worthy exploits and better than most, for instance, if a young nailmaker were to marry a collier she was considered as having married beneath herself according to (Owen 1989):

"Daughters of nailers who sought a collier for a husband were seen as traitors and deserters. Colliers, though better paid, were unskilled and beholden to other men."

Wherever there is money to made at the expense of others, one will always find others, willing to exploit the hard labours of the former in order to turn a quick profit. This is true of any 'sweated' or homeworking industry Hutchins (1907) quoting the House of Lords Committee defines sweating as:

1. – Unduly low rates of wages.
2. – Excessive hours of labour.
3. – Insanitary state of the workplaces.

There were many such industries, covering the Black Country and the Birmingham area. Anywhere that there were people or families willing to do anything just to survive, sweating would proliferate. Some historians have tried to focus on the evil of the sweated industry as something that had died out in Birmingham with the advent of municipalisation, yet continued to exist in the Black Country. In Cadbury and Shann (1907) their book entitled 'Sweating' the evidence is damning that sweating was far from over in Birmingham it had merely been hidden in the urban sprawl, they write:

"In Birmingham the chief of the unskilled home trades is carding and hooks and eyes. It is said that a machine has been invented to do this work, but as yet the cheapness of the human machine has hindered the general introduction of the workers' mechanical rival."

The reference to unskilled trades is noted, yet chainmaking was skilled, so how did it manage to become sweated, and why were the workers allowing themselves to become sweated? The answer lies with the middlemen and women, the foggers. Cadbury and Shann (1907) call them the small masters. In 'The White Slaves of England' by Sherard (1898) he refers directly to the Cradley Heath chainmaking when he describes the abundance of foggers, the majority of which were women who had never had to toil, yet earned a healthy living from those that were forced to do so by them. Again, Hutchins

(1907) in her tract for The Fabian Society, entitled 'Home Work and Sweating – The causes and the remedies', explains why the foggers (the sweater) survives so well:

"Although, broadly speaking, the factory is the more economical method, yet the employment of home-workers offers an advantage, in that very little capital is needed for starting or extending a business, and also because the sweating employer or contractor is able to shift some of the cost on to other people's shoulders. The manufacturer has to pay rent and rates for his factory; the sweater leaves the workers to pay rent for themselves. The manufacturer has to observe Factory Act requirements as to the cleaning, ventilation and sanitation of his factory; the sweater does not trouble about the condition of his workrooms to which he gives out work, as long as he gets the work done."

This was very true of Cradley Heath and the surrounding areas. The factory owners needed to supply large contracts with smaller items, but they were not willing to give up the valuable factory space where the larger items were manufactured, to do so. Also, the additional workers would have to be paid the same wages. It was far easier to work with, and in, the fogger system. The fogger supplied the iron and in many cases the forge premises and tools to the chainmaker. The chainmaker then had to make so much chain within a week, usually greatly exceeding factory hours, if less chain came back than should, fines and deductions were made from the payment. After they received their pay, they had to pay the fogger for rent, and they had to buy their fuel, food, etc. This way the fogger could keep insisting on keeping wages low, or even lowering them further.

When times got hard for the fogger, because a recession would mean that fewer chains were being ordered, they would cut the wages or even refuse to pay the workers. Most of the foggers had other businesses, small shops or alehouses. When they would not pay in money they would pay in kind, usually unsaleable goods of poor quality. Some poor souls were forced into penury as a consequence, and would have to approach the fogger for a loan. This was when the fogger would push their exploitation of their workers to the extreme; they would grant the loan, but they would set interest rates too high, and as a consequence the chainmaker would default, and then find themselves quite literally enslaved to the fogger; working for nothing for the rest of their lives.

With this system in place it is not hard to see how easy it was to continue to capitalise on the sweat of the impoverished workforce. If you were paid less one week and approached the fogger to ask for more, you would simply be told there would be more people to take your place and to put up with it. As chainmaking existed very much in isolation with little or no time to socialise, the women would not have much opportunity, to organise themselves (as their men had done previously) to make protest. Especially as the women, were doing at least two jobs, in some cases three; chainmaker, homemaker, mother.

As Hutchins (1907) notes this was not a novelty of the time, sweating of the workers had existed as long as anyone could remember:

"Sweating is no new thing. It occurs usually as a symptom of one of two kinds of industrial change: either as the decay of a handicraft or as an extension or offshoot of the factory system."

In the case of chainmaking it was the latter, the factory owners were not interested in the conditions of the outsourced workers, they merely wanted their stockrooms full to meet the orders. This allowed the foggers to perpetuate their exploitations, so that they too, could achieve the profit margins that they needed. It was easy, those who were left to do this work were grateful, it was the only work they could do, the only work that they knew how to do, and it kept some food on the table. The life of these women was a hard one and from the evidence had existed this way for at least two or three generations. Sherard (1898) describes the conditions of one such poor soul, known as Mrs D:

"I have known Mrs D for nearly ten years, and have found her to be thoroughly honest and would be a respectable woman, as she comes from a respectable family. But what with bad trade she was nearly brought to starvation some time ago."

He continues:

"...and when her children's stockings wanted washing, she had to put them to bed, for none of them 'had more than one bit to his feet'. The washing was usually done on Saturday evenings, when she had finished her work."

One can only begin to imagine, how difficult a life it was for a woman working full time in heavy manual work, trying to raise her family without enough money to buy more than one pair of stockings for each of her children; having to set all her household tasks into time periods after she had finished a full day. This was a situation that persisted because of the need for the woman to work and continued for years, as Cadbury and Shann (1907) describe the industry in Cradley:

"It is because so many of the men are wasteful that the women have to work. A woman is expected to work, and a man looks out for a wife that can work...The children look dirty but not unhealthy. Possibly, the comparatively healthy condition of these children is due to the fact that only the stronger ones survive, as the infant mortality is high."

I am going to endeavour to piece together from a handful of different accounts the life of a chainmaker. Most of these anecdotes come from the actual time of (or just before) the Cradley Heath strike of 1910, though other descriptions herald from other examples of historical research at an earlier date. It does not seem to matter when these histories were recorded for nothing had changed in the women's favour, in fact, the working conditions were deteriorating year on year. This was the description given by Gertrude Tuckwell (1910) of the expectations of production that were put on the women prior to the dispute:

"The women in the trade are practically all outworkers and the chains on which they labour is known as hand hammered. It consists very largely of cow-ties, horse traces, gate chains, and a variety of other chains on which no great strain has to be placed. Of these women there are nearly 2,000, and until the coming of the Chain Board all, save a very few who were given specially fine work to do, may be said to have been badly sweated.

At a meeting held in the beginning of last year attended by several hundreds of the women, it was asked from the platform if any of them made on the average more than 7/- a week. Not one woman claimed that she made so much. Only a few were found to average 6/-, and the great mass of those present averaged less than 5/-.

The amounts are the more incredible when the nature of their work is considered. The women take the iron from their employers' yard or they have it conveyed to them. Sometimes it is taken on the back of a woman; sometimes in a small barrow, and, of course, it may have to be conveyed a short or great distance. Each woman has her own forge, possibly two or three forges, in a sort of out-house which faces the backdoor of the house in which she lives. Workers are here employed to the number of forges. A women may work solitarily. If, as is in the case with most of the Cradley women, she is a mother, her children will sooner or later be found a place in the "shop". This explains how many of the women who are widows or who receive no aid from their husbands, have been able to exist. The woman herself has been able to earn but a few shillings. The sum earned by different members of her family may yield enough to, at any rate, keep the house going and its residents alive.

The normal weekly consumption of iron by a woman of average strength and quickness, making the very commonest chain, and working from 40 to 50 hours, will be about 2 cwt. of iron. Out of this she will make something less than the same amount of chain, the leakage of material being about 12 lbs. on the cwt. For chain of such quality she would get under the old conditions 3/3, 3/6, 3/9, or possibly 4/- per cwt. of chain made. According as the price rose, her output would fall off. In the best chains for which considerably high prices are paid, the weeks work wuld (sic) probably not yield more than ½ cwt of chain." "As has been said, it was found that 5/- for the great majority of women was an average wage, for from their gross earnings of 6/-, 7/- or 8/-, 2/- or 2/6 had to be deducted for the rent of their shops."

She paints a very bleak picture of the sheer drudgery that each woman faced in order to make but a few shillings a week to eek out a paltry living. The hours that had to be applied to the task of chainmaking, and the amounts of chain that had to be produced, were exceptionally long and arduous, especially if one considers the responsibilities of childcare and housewifery that were on her shoulders, there was little wonder that the children were dirty, she had little time left to take care of them. This had changed little from Sherard's account (1898) where he describes Mrs D having to make chain at '5s. 4d the cwt.' and to managing to 'work twelve hours a day, she could make about one cwt.'

The children would be watched by their mothers in the forge. It was the only way that mothers could combine the roles, and as Sherard (1898) records they used to find very ingenious ways of dealing with small infants:

"In a shed, fitted with a forge and anvil, there was a woman at work. From a polo (sic) which ran across the room there dangled a tiny swing chair for the baby, so that whilst working her hammers, the mother could rock the child."

This was not an uncommon practice and was even found recorded in an inventory of 1690 according to Moss (1977), who when speaking to old contemporary chainmakers of his time, recorded this historical practice continuing well into the twentieth century.

It was a dangerous occupation for the women, many of whom were scarred and blistered from the flying sparks of the forge. Their left hands tended to fair worse as they used the tongs with this hand, and their right hands which wielded the hammer were generally smoother and less scarred. Having children there too, particularly small ones, must have been highly stressful, a description by Sherard (1898) describes this in detail:

"The impediment of children, to mothers to whom motherhood is hero (sic) a curse, is nowhere more clearly defined. The wretched women, forging link by link the heavy chain, of which she must make 1 cwt. before her weekly rent is paid, is at each moment harassed by her sons and daughters. There is one child at her breast, who hampers the swing of the arm; there is another seated on the forge, who must be watched lest the too comfortable blaze at which it warms its little naked feet, prove dangerous, whilst the swarm that cling to her tattered skirt break the instinctive movement of her weary feet."

And fatalities were often recorded. I have included in the appendices an account from the great-granddaughter of a Cradley Heath chainmaker, unabridged. In this Yvonne Routledge describes the hard existence of her great grandmother – Rebecca. Yvonne draws our attention to the family story that one of her grandmother's brothers died probably from burns after falling into the forge.

When Mary Macarthur wrote her article 'Slaves to the Forge' to bring the cause to the public's attention in 1910, she shows her distress at what she considers to be the 'saddest of all Cradley sights':

"Just now in Cradley several pretty girls are beginning drear apprenticeship. I think of one especially, a slim gentle girl, whom a few days ago I saw panting over her forge. Already she can make her hundredweight of 'slap' a week. 'Some day,' she said, proudly, 'I shall be able to make two hundredweight.'"

At fourteen years old, girls were expected to assume their lives in the forge, to work, week on week, producing their two hundredweight of chain. That would entail 'shutting' 5,000 links per week, which required 10 blows of the hammer, as Macarthur stresses, 50,000 blows of the hammer a week.

Very quickly these young girls became amazons in appearance and were described as such. In earlier times, particularly in summer months when the forge was blisteringly hot, women were often to be found to have removed their upper clothing; bare-breasted at the forge, risking even greater bodily injury for blessed relief from the unremitting heat. Their bodies had become so muscular from their toil, that to some they bore a frightening appearance, not the vision of weak-Victorian, or Edwardian, womanhood, a very challenge to discourse of feminine acceptability. In Sherard's (1898) account he describes a group of such women working in one forge:

"...they are all talking above the din of their hammers and clanking of their chains, or they may be singing a discordant chorus; and at first, the sight of this sociability makes one overlook the misery, which, however, is only too visible, be it in the foul rags and the preposterous boots that the women wear, or in their haggard faces and the faces of the wizened infants hanging to their mothers' breasts, as these ply the hammer, or sprawling in the mire on the floor, amidst a shower of fiery sparks."

Their children were often born between breaks in their work, quite literally having to give birth and then returning hours later. They had to, without their relentless endeavours, all would all starve.

It is often written that many lived to remarkable ages, whether that is because the of Darwinian survival of the fittest – with only those infants strong enough to survive being themselves – or because the relentless work kept them fitter than the average well-to-do woman; trussed up in the physically damaging corsets, unable to exercise. Their longevity certainly had very little to do with their diet, which was usually very meagre; bread being the staple food for most, supplemented by some meat, which was necessary to keep up the heavy, manual labour, day after day.

One of the characters of the strike, much used by the NFWW in their publicity efforts was Patience Round. At the time of the strike she was seventy-nine years old and one of the oldest of the women. She was interviewed extensively by the newspapers. In one account she is recorded as saying:

"In the whole of my life I have never stopped working in the shop for more than two days. I started when I was a little girl of ten – it seems long, long years ago now – and ever since then, I have made chains hundreds and hundreds of miles of them. Once I used to count, and counted up to 3,000 miles, but that was long ago.

I have learned to love the forge, for in the winter the glowing fire keeps me warm, and the bright sparks keep me cheerful; I am getting just a little old now. My husband is a cripple, and it is hard work to keep our little home together."

One can only begin to imagine what it must have been like for Patience having worked nearly seventy years at the same arduous toil; raising her family, with all of the prevailing dangers, and trying to make enough, to bring sufficient money into the home, to keep food on the table. And then in the evenings when she stopped working, trying to find the time to carry out the tasks of a normal wife and mother. As the years went on, and her husband became invalided, to face the prospect that she had to continue and never stop or they both would be starving and homeless. Finally, with her eightieth birthday approaching, with the full knowledge that she must always keep going until she dropped dead at the forge.

Chapter 5

THOSE THAT TRIED TO MAKE A DIFFERENCE

In this chapter, I will outline the key characters who were most influential in the establishing of the Trade Boards that helped to set the minimum wage, and particularly those who helped to promote the cause of the striking women in Cradley Heath. I shall not discuss Mary Macarthur here, as she has had enormous impact on the recording and reporting of the history, I will discuss her in more detail in the ensuing chapter.

As briefly discussed in the first chapter, there was a movement of socially philanthropic individuals who sought to make change through discussion and writing; these people helped to create the discourse for the need for action for those who were impoverished and disadvantaged. There were both men and women from similar backgrounds, well-educated, upper middle class, and generally liberal in their politics; though as the socialist movement grew in its appeal and magnitude, many changed their allegiances. I have already mentioned briefly, Clementina Black, Beatrice Webb (nee Potter), Margaret MacDonald (nee Gladstone), but the list can be added to extensively. The people that concern this story profoundly are; Lady Emilia Dilke (nee Strong), Sir Charles Wentworth Dilke MP, Gertrude Tuckwell, James Joseph Mallon, Julia Varley, Thomas Sitch and his son Charles, and of course Mary Macarthur. On the periphery of this key group but still with a significant contribution are; Alfred George Gardiner, George Cadbury and his son Edward, Elizabeth Hutchins. Further, there were a group of influential politicians who helped to promote the various causes to a greater or lesser extent; Keir Hardie MP, Arthur Henderson MP, William Anderson MP, Winston Churchill MP, David Lloyd George MP and Ramsay MacDonald MP. These were by far not the only people involved, but are those that feature most in the research archives. I will give a brief biography of each and place their involvement within this story.

As was true with the broader political picture, the need of having to encompass a wide spectrum of belief under one banner would invariably lead to disagreement and fallout, so was true of the various groups and societies who pushed for reform. Although they, for the most part, had the same final goals in most cases, how to reach those goals and what strategy to take was often the cause of much disagreement. As beliefs hardened, so a stance would become rigidly entrenched often leading to disputes amongst key members which could not be resolved. Two such beacons of change, who ended up disagreeing strongly were Clementina Black and Margaret MacDonald.

Clementina Black was born in 1853, according to Grenier (2004) she was known as a writer, political activist and suffragist. When her father was widowed and an invalid, it fell on Clementina's shoulders to support the family, this she did through her writing. Her personal interests were shaped by her living in London and associating with the various intellectual discussion groups including the Fabians and Marxists. She was particularly driven to improve the rights of workers, especially women, through the concept of trade unionism and was made secretary of the Women's Protective and Provident League (whose founder Emma Paterson was to go on to found the Women's Trade Union League, which would feature in this story). She became actively involved in the Match Girls' strike in 1889, which led to her belief that only a radical approach to trade unionism would solve the underlying problems of sweating. She too founded the Women's Trade Union Association, which although short lived, went on to form the Women's Industrial Council, where she would work alongside Margaret MacDonald.

Clementina believed that a minimum wage was the only way to alleviate many of the problems that she had experienced and witnessed, and from 1896 became politically active in the pursuit of this cause. She wrote extensively on the subject, pursuing vigorous lines of enquiry and debate in order to raise public awareness. When the executive committee of the National Anti-Sweating league was formed she sat on this. She was forced to resign her position from the WIC, following an ideological split (probably with Margaret MacDonald) over her insistence on the need to set a statutory minimum wage, after the Trade Boards Act was passed in 1909.

Margaret MacDonald was born in 1870 – in considerably better circumstances than Clementina – in London, and brought up in a Liberal household (Hannam 2004). By the 1890's, through her various teaching and secretarial activities, she had been exposed to many of the harsh conditions that she would campaign on behalf of, she also mixed in similar circles as those that Clementina preferred. She became active in the WIC, and met and eventually married (James) Ramsay Macdonald, the would-be future Prime Minister of the first Labour Government.

Margaret believed that the way to improve the plight of the poor under-privileged women, was through better education and training, but probably from her religious beliefs, she was strongly against married women's paid employment. This led her into conflict with those organisations which were trying to organise women, such as the WTUL. It was probably the issue that caused Clementina Black's resignation from the WIC. Margaret disagreed with the Trade Boards Bill, and set her cap against it, as most others I will refer to here did not.

At the same time, Margaret was highly active in the National Union of Women Workers, which can be viewed as the sister organisation to the WTUL but with opposing views on the employment of married women. She did help to found, and was president of – before her untimely death of blood poisoning in 1911 – the Women's Labour League. This was an organisation dedicated to encourage women's involvement in socialist politics.

It is very problematic to discuss Beatrice Webb (nee Potter) born 1858, without reference to her husband Sydney Webb (1859), for the two always operated in a partnership and are viewed as two of the leading social scientists of their day (Davis 2004). They were the key influences on many of those forming their beliefs and understanding, although as a couple they were so different in background. Beatrice was born into affluence and educated substantially above the norms of female Victorian society. She was well-schooled in philosophical thinking, which placed her in a very different sphere to that of her contemporaries. She was said to be a very spiritual person, but rejected religion in favour of a belief of some deeper guiding force. Her cousin by marriage was Charles Booth, and her father introduced her to other intellectual thinkers of the day.

In 1883, she was to be confronted by severe infatuation for a man twenty years her senior, which was to continue to impact on her mental and emotional stability even long after she was married. She was introduced to Joseph Chamberlain MP, who cut a dash in society with his good looks and charisma. However strongly attracted to him that she was, she was repelled by his subordinating attitudes to women and although he had shown her some attentions, he was that much older and twice widowed and not actively seeking romance or companionship, merely a marriage partner.

Beatrice was a great thinker and writer, and she carried out various social science investigations to observe poverty in real life. These studies brought her to the conclusions that the problems in society required actual remedies, not treatment (Davis 2004). In 1890 she met Sydney Webb, a man from a lesser background who physically she was not attracted to, but intellectually she had found him to be her equal. The pair eventually married after her father's death, and because of their mutual research projects and writing, they became the beacon for many in the study of social change. They dominated the Fabian Society for nearly fifty years (Davis 2004). They founded the London School of Economics together in the 1890's and wrote extensively on the subject of trade unionism.

Lady Emilia Dilke born in 1840 (Francis Emilia Strong), was a contemporary of all three of these women mentioned previously. She hailed from a reasonably affluent background in Devon, and because of the artistic circles that her parents associated with, she was encouraged by John Ruskin to go to London and study design (Fraser 2004). After which she married for the first time, Mark Pattison, and became a rector's wife in Lincoln pursuing her love of art through writing. She became involved with the Women's Protective and Provident League (later to be the WTUL) under the auspices of Emma Paterson. In 1884 her first husband died, and the following year, she married her old acquaintance, Sir Charles Wentworth Dilke. With the death of Emma Paterson in 1886, Emilia became the president of the WTUL.

Emilia rehabilitated Charles within society, after he had suffered some public humiliation in a divorce case scandal. They were highly supportive of one another, both in their ideals and campaigning. Much of what Emilia was trying to do through her role in the WTUL, Charles would bring into the House of Commons and formed a circle of committed like-minded MPs. Unfortunately, Lady Emilia was not to live to see the famous Cradley Heath victory in which her protégé Mary Macarthur would lead, she died in 1904, but Sir Charles would continue on, leading the vanguard for the Trade Boards Bill.

Gertrude Tuckwell was the niece of Lady Emilia Dilke. Gertrude was born in 1861 in Oxford, she was said to have had her greatest influences from her aunt (John, 2004). She trained as a teacher, and in 1893 became labour secretary to her aunt. She began to write in earnest about social welfare, as a direct result of living with Emilia – who had remarried by this time – she found the whole environment intellectually stimulating. When Emilia Dilke assumed the presidency of the WTUL, Gertrude became the honorary secretary; it was these two women who interviewed Mary Macarthur for the position of secretary after the retirement of Mona Wilson. Gertrude was to become president of the league in 1905 following the death of her aunt, and would eventually be president of the satellite organisation, the National Federation of Women Workers founded by Mary Macarthur (the union that would fight the Cradley Heath cause).

Gertrude was a founder of the National Anti-Sweating League, and gave evidence to the 1907 Select Committee on Homework. She sat on the Executive Committee of the International Association for Labour Legislation, and when she founded the British section, Sidney Webb became chairman (John 2004). Gertrude remained active until 1930, although she retired from trade unionism in 1918. She was a great archivist and it is thanks to her extensive collection of papers at the Trades Union Congress Library, that we are fortunate to be able to read much of the documentation relating to the dispute.

Sir Charles Wentworth Dilke was born in 1843, and was the second baronet (Jenkins 2004). He had the young life of a normal aristocrat of his time, his years spent between extensive education and travelling. Finally, in the mid-1860's he was elected to Parliament as a Radical Liberal, there he struck up a friendship with Joseph Chamberlain who had been elected a few years later. Joseph needed the right contacts to help network in the elevated circles and Charles was attracted by the charismatic businessman, who had the weight of the Birmingham Liberal Caucus behind him, and the National Liberal Federation which Chamberlain had been instrumental in instigating. Dilke was always embroiled in thorny issues such as republicanism, and would make himself unpopular from time to time for airing his views. He was briefly married to his first wife in the early 1870's who died in childbirth.

This tragedy had a serious effect on him. After some deep grieving in Paris, he fell on the friendship of Emilia Pattison (nee Strong) for support and threw himself headlong into his political career, with Joseph Chamberlain as his main ally. Such a powerful team could not be ignored by Gladstone, who offered them one cabinet post between them, the Board of Trade, which was eventually headed by Joseph with Charles as under secretary at the Foreign Office. They were a pair with some standing in the government, but as was the nature of the Liberal party at that time, very often at odds with Gladstone who they perceived as not progressive.

In 1885 the Redistribution of Seats Bill proved to be a rocky time for the liberals, but Dilke pushed his bill through with the aid of Chamberlain as a team. At that time he had become recently engaged to Emilia Pattison, but all at once things turned sour for Charles Dilke. The government resigned en masse, some authors record that the disagreements regarding Irish Home Rule, caused by Chamberlain and Dilke, had precipitated disunity in the party. As if this was not enough, he was accused publically of having seduced a young married woman many years before, an allegation he most vehemently denied. Unfortunately, the ensuing divorce case did not call him to give a defence, because none of the allegations were submitted as evidence in court. Charles Dilke was then forced by the press to defend his position in due course, he probably realised that this would be ruinous, as it would be impossible to prove a negative. It all went terribly wrong for Sir Charles Dilke, whose reputation was permanently besmirched.

Emilia stood by him, and slowly he rebuilt his political career, though never to the levels that it had been. Many friends deserted him, as he had become a political pariah, however he worked tirelessly on the minimum wage, which was Emilia's mission. After Emilia's death in 1904, he never really regained his previous strength, she had been his rock.

Julia Varley born in 1871, had such a different life to all those mentioned so far. She was from the working classes and very much so. At the age of twelve she had left school and started as a weaver in the Bradford cotton mills (Doughan 2004). By the age of fifteen she was the branch secretary for the Weavers and Textiles Union in Bradford. She was forced to give up full time work on the death of her mother in order to care for the rest the family. She continued her union work, and became an active unionist as a consequence. She made studies of the school meals provision, and she sat on the Bradford Board of Guardians.

From this she decided to make a study of tramping women, many of whom she had come into contact with through her duties on the board. This led her to disguise herself as one and live amongst them for a while, which in turn brought her to London. She claimed that she had been a suffragette and locked up in Holloway prison on a couple of occasions.

By 1907 she had met Mary Macarthur and been introduced to the work of the National Federation of Women Workers. Mary had invited her to take a position, as one of the area organisers that the NFWW needed, the patch that Julia was given was Birmingham and the Black Country. It is likely that Julia's attention was drawn to Cradley Chainmakers by others such as Gertrude Tuckwell, she threw herself into the task of trying to recruit as many as she could to the union. After the dispute ended, she was invited by Edward Cadbury to organise the women at Cadbury's in Bournville. She set up a branch in Birmingham which became affiliated to the Birmingham Trades Council (Doughan 2004).

Within a few years, she changed her allegiances away from the NFWW to the Workers Union, Julia believed strongly that men and women should be organised in the same union and this put her at odds with the work of the NFWW. She did remain in the Birmingham and Black Country area, where she had made her home in Hay Lane until the 1930's.

Thomas Sitch and Charles Sitch (father and son), were the local unionists who led the Chainmakers. Thomas Sitch had been born in Cradley Heath in 1852, but had moved to Newcastle with his parents, and then to Chester. In 1889 he founded the Chainmakers' and Strikers' Association of Saltney near Chester (Taylor 2004). He became very successful representing the factory workers, who were of course mainly men. After his son Charles was born, he moved back to Cradley Heath and continued his union work vigorously.

Charles was born in 1887 and by the late 1890's with support from the union, he was able to able to attend Ruskin College in Oxford to study Economics. When he returned to Cradley he was fired up with union work, particularly for those that for the most part had been unrepresented, the hand hammered branch. In other words, the women who worked in the back street forges for very little money. Once the NFWW began to recruit, he and Mary Macarthur worked hard on raising public awareness of the plight of the women, which eventually led to the setting up of the Trade Boards which settled the minimum wage and precipitated the strike.

As branch secretary of the hand hammered section, Charles Sitch played a key role in the dispute, and as with Julia Varley, were the two that did the most in terms of day-to-day organising. Charles continued as an active unionist for some years after, representing other trades, such as, the hollowware workers. He became a Labour MP in 1916 and was elected in 1918 staying in the House until 1931, his father died in 1923 at Unity Villa, Sydney Road, Cradley Heath. In 1933 Charles was convicted of obtaining funds through deception and sentenced to nine months in prison. After which he moved to Leeds, where he remained until his death in 1960 of pulmonary tuberculosis.

James Joseph Mallon (b. 1874) is one who emphasises the web of friends that interacted to a great extent; he was affectionately known as 'Father O'Flynn' in later years. He was born in Manchester to Irish Catholic parents, and after the death of his father, became an apprentice jeweller, which led him into the Shop Assistants Union (Briggs 2004). While studying at university in Manchester, he became committed into helping the under-privileged working class, eventually moving to the East End of London in 1905. He had already been a member of the Fabian Society for two years. It was at this time he began to work closely with Mary Macarthur, firstly on the Anti-Sweating Exhibition and then with the establishment of the National

Anti-Sweating League. He was passionate about the need to establish a minimum wage, and became an active campaigner.

On the passage of the Trades Board Act in 1909, he was to sit as honorary treasurer of the Trade Boards Advisory Council, and in fact, he was a member of thirteen of the first trade boards that were established. The next person that I am going to introduce to you is A. G. Gardiner, the editor of the Daily News, James Joseph Mallon was to marry his daughter, Stella Gardiner, in 1921.

Alfred George Gardiner was born in Essex in 1865. After an apprenticeship in journalism locally, he moved to the north of England where he worked for the Northern Daily Telegraph. He quickly rose to editor and was known for his non-conformist, anti-imperialist stance and very liberal views (Morris 2004).

George Cadbury was encouraged by David Lloyd George to purchase The Daily News in London (once the paper of Charles Dickens). The Liberal Party needed an organ that was a direct challenge to the Conservative views being expressed in The Times, The Daily News became that mouthpiece. A. G. Gardiner was appointed as editor in 1902 with no previous Fleet Street experience (Morris 2004). At first, he was in tune with the Liberal voice, however, his views became too outspoken and radical for Lloyd George, and unprintable for Cadbury who was a devout Quaker.

Alfred Gardiner, was a great supporter of the Anti-Sweating Exhibition, and the handbook for that exhibition was published by The Daily News. It was no wonder that there should be so much financial support for the exhibition, because either he persuaded George Cadbury to donate the lion's share of sponsorship, or Cadbury initiated that himself. However, as a Quaker, Cadbury did not support trade unionism and although he would have supported the National Anti-Sweating League and Mary Macarthur's involvement in that, it probable to assume that he would not have been so supportive of his newspapers high profile support for the NFWW and their involvement in the Cradley Heath strike.

George Cadbury was born in Edgbaston, Birmingham in 1839. His father John had established a cocoa manufacturing enterprise, and George with his elder brother Richard developed the business further; while at the same time building a Quaker community in Bournville for their workers. George was left solely in charge in 1899 when Richard died, the business had developed from employing 20 people to 8,600 (Williams 2004).

George was a great believer in Adult Education and good religious teaching and gave many of his own hours to running adult education classes.

He was against all war, and found the Boer War particularly abhorrent and when he was encouraged by Lloyd George to become proprietor of The Daily News, he used his paper to promote anti-war rhetoric.

His son Edward was one of the leading social researchers of his time, investigating women in the manufacturing workforce, and the issues of sweating. Birmingham and the Black Country, provided ample opportunity to carry out detailed research with his co-authors George Shann and Cecile Matheson. He would record the results of his findings, and compare them against his own experiences of managing the female workers in his father's company.

Both Edward and his father showed their support for the Cradley strike by donating to the strike fund for the non-organised women. Edward was gracious enough to come and give a speech to the strikers at the Empire Theatre, however, he did acknowledge in that speech that he did not hold with unions, but he strongly believed that the Cradley women were fighting for what he considered to be most important cause for all sweated workers.

Elizabeth Hutchins was a social researcher who was born in 1858, she was privately educated before attending King's College for Women in London and then in 1896 the London school of Economics (Malone 2004). She became a member of the Women's Industrial Council and in 1904 and was elected to the executive. She was an active member in the Fabian Society, and an executive member from 1907 to 1912.

One of the main topics of her extensive research into women's labour and conditions of work, was that of sweated labour. She wrote an article on the Berlin Anti-Sweating Exhibition, before making a significant contribution to the handbook produced for the London exhibition of the following year (published by The Daily News). From this she later produced a tract for the Fabian Society upon the subject entitled; 'Homework and Sweating: the causes and remedies'.

Throughout her career as a social researcher, she took issue with those women's groups who were determined to maintain objection to married women working, or who did little to promote the cause to improving working conditions of those employed. As such she drew closer to WTUL (Clementina Black and Mary Macarthur in particular) whom she viewed as being most pragmatic in their approach.

There was a complex web of political personalities who were involved in the movement for the establishment of the Trade Boards and the minimum wage. Three I have mentioned already, Sir Charles Dilke MP descriptively, Ramsay MacDonald MP and David Lloyd George MP briefly. I believe that it is important to note that political views are not set in stone and can sometime switch allegiance based on experience, and/or self-interest, of the politicians mentioned here, this could certainly be said in the case of two of them, Lloyd George and Winston Churchill. Unlike the others that I have reviewed till now, I will only discuss their lives up till the time of the strike, as they all had extensive careers after the Cradley Heath dispute.

David Lloyd George was born in Manchester in 1863, due to the influences of his Welsh uncle Richard Lloyd, David's path to politics was never in doubt (K. O. Morgan 2004). He very quickly became one of the hot young liberals of his day, taking issue with anything that was seen to be a stagnation within the liberal politics and emanating from the Gladstonian camp. In his need to be an opposing voice, he aligned himself with Joseph Chamberlain's revolt of the Irish Home Rule Bill in 1886, which caused the split of the Radical Unionists led by Chamberlain challenging their own party. However in later years, Lloyd George was to actively oppose Chamberlain, whom he saw as starting the Boer War out of self-interest (Chamberlain was Colonial Secretary at the time), and profiteering from it through his family's interest in the small-arms manufacturing sector in Birmingham.

At that time, he had persuaded George Cadbury to acquire The Daily News, as much for David Lloyd George's own personal career advancement, as for the pronouncements against 'jingoism' and imperialism (K. O. Morgan 2004). He was also one to make his opinions known loudly, and had to learn by his own mistakes when and where to do this. An incident of the public meeting in Birmingham's town hall, where he spoke against 'the great municipaliser' (Chamberlain), who had renovated a decaying town into a great city, was not Lloyd George's most sensible of debates. It led to such a public outrage from the assembled crowd, that he had to be smuggled out in an ill-fitting policeman's uniform.

He continued to oppose Chamberlain on tariff reform, and was considered a supporter of free-trade. He came into the cabinet in 1906 as president of the Board of Trade, with no previous experience. He showed remarkable ability to handle this position at a difficult time of rising civil disputes and unrest. This was the beginning of a love-hate relationship with the unions, as a liberal he knew of the need for real reforms and one of his most acclaimed achievements was that of the contribution to the Pensions Bill, and later the National Insurance Bill. But what could have been viewed by some as generous, was viewed by others as not generous enough. When he had to put down the various industrial disputes he was seen as being hard, yet he was also acclaimed for his negotiations in the railway strike.

He was president of the Board of Trade just prior to Trades Board Bill, which his successor Winston Churchill would be credited with. On one or two occasions, he has been noted to have crossed swords with Mary Macarthur, after the Cradley dispute, whom he considered to be immature and too hysterical. She was pressing for more for her under-privileged women in the health insurance proposals, he as Chancellor of the Exchequer was trying to balance the books, I believe it is fair to surmise that they were two equally strong characters, not prepared to compromise; each one failing to fall for the reported fateful charm of the other.

Winston Churchill was born in 1874, at Blenheim Palace in Oxfordshire. His father was Lord Randolph Churchill, the notable Member of Parliament and Jennie Churchill (nee Jerome) an American socialite and heiress. Winston was determined to do something with his life, and had a driven desire to make his father proud (whom he lost to debilitating illness thought to have been syphilis, though now suspected as a brain tumour) (Addison 2004).

After passing out of Sandhurst and being posted to India and then onto the Sudan, doubling as a war correspondent he wrote a number of books which were critical of campaign leadership. Finally he went out as a correspondent and army officer during the Boer War, where he was first interned and then managed to escape, his progress through South Africa was reported daily in the British newspapers, particularly the Morning Post, to which he was contracted. His successful flight to Durban brought him the fame he was seeking, his next ambition was to build his political career.

At first he stood as his father had for the Conservatives, and because of the publicity that he had gained, won a victory in the constituency of Oldham. With the change of leadership from Lord Salisbury to his nephew Arthur Balfour in 1902, Churchill found that his career was not advancing as fast as he would have hoped. He was uncomfortable with Joseph Chamberlain's, campaign for tariff reform, and set himself firmly in the camp for 'free trade'. The Conservative party was seemingly falling apart with disunity and disagreement, on 31st May 1904, Churchill crossed the House and sat next to his good friend Lloyd George, signalling his change of allegiance to the Liberal brethren.

Under the auspices of Liberalism he made good progress, becoming one of the youngest men to obtain cabinet office at 33 years old. Asquith appointed him as president of the Board of Trade, on which he was able to work closely with Lloyd George (who was by that time Chancellor of the Exchequer) on delivering some of the most revolutionary social reforms of the early twentieth century; the Trade Boards Bill in order to set the statutory minimum wage, the establishment of Labour Exchanges and the infant National Insurance Bill. All of which had to be financed, and the two argued the case for cutting the defence budget, positing the position of a lasting peace with Germany.

Churchill was a great personal friend of Lloyd George, and when the latter put forward the People's Budget of 1909 which was received with hostility by many, Churchill became proactive in his defence through a campaign of speeches and publicity. Churchill was in agreement with the need to abolish sweated work, he believed in the rights for women to vote, but disliked suffragettes. During the Great Unrest he was often criticised for using heavy-handed policing tactics to put down disputes.

James Keir Hardie (b. 1856, Lanarkshire, Scotland) is credited with founding the Labour party (K. O. Morgan 2004). From a very poor background, Hardie became a miner, who educated himself often by the light of a miner's lamp before commencing as a journalist in Glasgow; following this he became secretary of the Miners Union in Ayrshire. His understanding of Marxism and Liberalism led him to formulate his socialist ideology, which brought him to challenge the received political opinion of the day. By 1892 he had been returned to the House of Commons as an Independent Labour candidate.

The Labour Representation Committee came into being in 1899 with Hardie as the chairman, it was an alliance of the Trade Unions and various socialist societies. After losing his seat in the 'khaki election' of 1900, he was adopted by the mining community of Merthyr Tydfil and subsequently became leader of the new parliamentary labour party, while Ramsay MacDonald chaired the Independent Labour Party. Although, a fine politician and an ardent believer in socialism, Hardie lacked the skills to lead a cohesive party and for a long time the movement was factional, as much due to those who felt a strong attraction to the 'father of socialism', as any internal party strife.

Ramsay MacDonald another poor Scotsman, was born in Lossiemouth in 1866. His progress into socialism was first as a member of the Social Democratic Federation in Bristol. After moving to London, working for a while and joining the Fabian Society, he began actively writing about socialism and labour ideals in 1892. Shortly after, he proclaimed himself a member of Keir Hardie's new Labour party and his political career began in earnest (Marquand 2004). Although an ardent supporter of the ideology, he instinctively knew that real positive progression for the infant labour movement could only be gained through pact and compromise with the old party of Liberals. However that is not to say, that if he strongly disagreed with something he would not make a stand, as he had done by resigning from the Fabian Society in protest when they refused to condemn the Boer War. The growth of the party and the unity was in most part due to his hard work and determination in trying to counteract any factionalism.

He married Margaret MacDonald (nee Gladstone) in 1896, and like the Webbs and the Dilkes, they were considered as a couple to be leading lights in social reform, until her tragic death in 1911. Ramsay never fully recovered from her loss, although he went on to be the first serving Labour prime minister.

Arthur Henderson was born in Glasgow in 1863, and was from an equally impoverished background to the previous two men. He left school at 12 and became an apprenticed iron-foundry man, during which time he joined the trade union and eventually became secretary of the Friendly Society of Iron Founders (Wrigley 2004). Due to the affiliation of that society to the LRC, Henderson found himself quite naturally drawn in the political spectrum of socialism. He was funded as a politician by the union until 1911 when MPs were then paid by the state (Wrigley 2004). He succeeded Hardie as chairman of the parliamentary labour party, and because of his collegiate attitude to political life he was considered to be more of a stable leader than his predecessor, who had been more inclined to erratic behaviour through his charismatic personality (Wrigley 2004).

Henderson was an avid supporter of the need for a minimum wage, and together with others such as David Shackleton MP, supported the WTUL and NFWW in their efforts to secure a victory at Cradley Heath.

William Crawford Anderson was born in 1877 in Banffshire Scotland, although not as impoverished as the previous three, his family were working class. He was apprenticed to an industrial chemist in Aberdeen, which led him into an active interest in trade unionism and radical politics (Melling 2004). After moving to Glasgow and joining the ILP, he stood in the Khaki election of 1900, with the backing of the Labour Party (Melling 2004).

His activities in trade unionism led him to take a full role in the Shop Assistants Union, which brought him into contact with Mary Macarthur. Their fond friendship and mutual attraction led to them marrying in 1911. Although his activities were primarily towards the ILP, he supported his future spouse in all of the campaigns that she led and because of his own charisma, attracted support from many others in the process. He was tipped as a future leader by those in his party, but unfortunately died in early 1919 from Spanish Influenza (Melling 2004).

This collection of individuals are comprehensively interlinked and form a network of those that were in the forefront of political and social philanthropy. That is not to say that they were the only individuals involved, as will become apparent in chapter 7. In any situation of this size and complexity, it is essential that there is a core of people who enable the change to happen; who bring the need for resolution into the public domain. The aforementioned individuals were part of other networks, who in turn assisted the progress towards the minimum wage. In Chapter 7 – 'By the sweat of their brow', their mutual endeavours on the campaign against sweating can bear witness to their cohesive strength to fight for the rights of those marginalised by commercialism of the late Victorian/early Edwardian society. In that chapter, many other prominent figures will be named who tied their colours to the mast to promote the cause for a minimum wage; this collective of like-minded people, in turn created a tidal wave of populace at large pushing for change.

Of all those associated with the strike, there is one name that stands out from all the rest, that of Mary Macarthur. Some may read this as her single-handed victory, as you will have read, this is far from the case for she was the tip of the iceberg that had been moving beneath her. She could not have been so successful without the massive support of others who worked tirelessly, she was just one of the many, but she would prove to be the most glorious.

Chapter 6

MARY REID MACARTHUR

By far the most significant personality of the strike was Mary Reid Macarthur, she has been honoured in history as being the key figure of influence on the successful outcome of the dispute. However, as I have already alluded to in the previous chapter, there were many others who had a role in this matter, and what I intend to show here is a balance to her involvement and why she has received much greater acclaim than others. That is not to say, that without her oratory skills and her ability to lead that it would have been settled, for I believe that she was the sort of catalytic person that was necessary to drive this on. Neither, do I believe that she intentionally, or deliberately, sought to achieve the public acclamation and status that the dispute elevated her to, for my research has led me to conclude that this was merely a side-effect of the whole story.

In this chapter I am going to introduce Mary Macarthur and give her background and experience that brought her to this point in 1910. I shall examine the set of circumstances that led her to undertake such an action, and who I consider to be the mentors that guided her on her path as a union activist. I will make a small consideration of her philosophies and ideals, also, her life after Cradley, which I believe has coloured the way that history sees her, and to a certain extent reveres her for this particular involvement.

As I have emphasised previously, all of this must be placed in the temporal context of the end of the nineteenth and the beginning of the twentieth century. Life for many, was altering unimaginably at a vastly accelerated rate, the pace of life was quickening and the new technologies were accelerating that pace of change indefinably. In fact, the new media and communication were between them creating vast cultural change, through their speed to deliver news and the accessibility of that news. I believe that it is the confluence of these and other factors, that have placed her centre stage.

History is a retrospective of what was believed to have occurred, it is only a truth if the validity of the accounts that build the story are accurate and available. So much was happening at a time of great upheaval not everything was recorded in this way for posterity. Although, there are extensive archives at the Trade Unions Congress Library in London, much is based on newspaper journalism, many of the more personal insights have been lost in time. A biography, written shortly after her death remains, but that too can have a colour of its own being written after such a life was cut prematurely short. However, when one pieces together all that has been written and recorded since, and the existing records of the time, then it is possible to reveal a more accurate picture, as I will attempt to do here.

Mary Reid Macarthur, or Molly as she was referred to by close friends and family, was born on the 13th August, 1880. She was the eldest of three girls, in a moderately well to-do family in Glasgow. Her father owned a chain of draperies and one in the West End. Not the inauspicious beginnings of many who found themselves drawn into union work. Her father prospered and as the chain grew, he moved his family to the Victorian exclusivity of the seaside town of Ayr, it was either there or Argyll where most prosperous Glasgow businessmen of his generation aspired to. There he had another large drapers and the family settled at Trabboch, their rural idyll. Mary was sent to finishing school in Germany, and upon her return, set to supporting her father in his business dealings. He was a Conservative and encouraged his daughter to participate in the Primrose League – the young conservatives – it is possible to speculate that he desired her to meet and marry 'one of their own kind'.

Mary was an intelligent young lady, with a considerable amount of internal drive, she was not the sort to sit idly at home or socialise. In 1897 she convinced her father to let her work for him in the Ayr store as his bookkeeper, it was there that she was to first become exposed to the real inequalities of human existence. She must have had opportunities to associate with his staff, the army of underpaid shop girls. By all accounts, Mr Macarthur was one of the better employers, but he still had a business to run and profits to make, so one can assume that he had girls 'living-in'.

As Margaret Bondfield of the Shop Assistants Union (who was to become one of Mary's closest friends) would never stop to protest about, 'living-in' was the curse of many poor girls. The conditions were often overcrowded and insanitary, girls were not just exposed to this but corrupting factors of older women living there who made money through less savoury activities, in order to supplement their pitiful income.

There is no doubt that things were not quite that bad for those that worked for Mary's father, but it would not be hard to believe that they were certainly able to recount such tales to Mary, who seems to have had a gift at being able to relate to others not of her social standing. By the following year after commencing her employment with her father, Mary was attending the Shop Assistants Union branch meetings in Ayr. She became very active in the union and by 1901 she had come to attention of one of the Union leaders; she made such a strong impression on John Turner that he recorded his thoughts in writing.

Mary's interest in all things connected with unionism grew quickly, this must have been driven by her sense of outrage at the conditions that she was learning about from others and her access to the union meetings. We must also remember, that this was the time that socialism was rising significantly, especially in the area that Mary lived. Kier Hardie had worked with the miners in Ayr and written and self-published journals, from there he would go on to give rise to the infant labour movement in Glasgow with other notables such as; Robert Smillie and Ramsay MacDonald. All of Mary's forming political thoughts and ideals, must have been affected by this groundswell of socialist undercurrent that was happening. It was also the time that she would first meet the man she would eventually marry, Will Anderson, an active Labour man.

At home, life must have become increasingly difficult for her, as she formed her strong outspoken opinions, to her equally strong outspoken father. Her political associations must have caused him great personal embarrassment, a situation that must have been exacerbated with her election as the Scottish National District President. All of those that were not the closest of associates with her father, would be more than aware of her conflicting views. It was at this time she is recorded as making one her first profound observations:

"Women are badly paid and badly treated because they are not organised, and they cannot organise because they are badly treated"

At this point, although she was working for a co-sexed union, she had already identified in her own mind, that women suffered greater inequalities at the hands of their employers, than did the men that they worked alongside.

The next glimpse that we get of Mary, reveals to us another important aspect of her personality. As Scottish president, Mary led the Scottish delegation to the National Conference of the Shop Assistants Union in Newcastle in 1902, there she met Margaret Bondfield for the first time, who described her as a 'tall, slim, radiant girl.' Indeed by all accounts, she was statuesque and blonde, so different from those others in the union (mainly men) who had worked up from the shop floor most likely. Her appearance would have been enough to draw each and everyone's attention to her, but that was not enough for Mary, she had to make a visual statement, and she arrived in a light, green, plaid dress. In her tartan, it was her statement that the Scottish had arrived, that Mary Macarthur was leading them.

Her father must have been further taken aback, by her bringing her new-found union friend, back to the family home straight after the conference; the strains must have been growing on the family. Some time during that year, Will Anderson made his first proposal of marriage to Mary. Whether this was rejected due to her youth, or in deference to her father, or because her passions for unionism were taking hold of her life, is unclear, in my opinion it was a combination of all these factors. Mary had no intention of being tied into wedlock too soon.

According to Arthur Henderson, who was to become one of the first Labour MPs, she made an approach to him to act as his secretary, something that she was advised against, for fear it might anger her father further.

She returned the following year to the National Conference, this time it was held in Manchester. There she greatly impressed many with her speeches and presence, she utilised her own experience and skills to openly criticise the union's financial management, this led her to J. J. Mallon's attention. Sometime shortly after the conference, Mary made the decision to leave Ayr for London. It is easy to speculate that she now felt uncomfortable in her home environment, and considered that it would be better moving away, whether she left on good or bad terms with her father is also unclear, although she did make a few visits back later. I believe that Mary had simply outgrown Ayr and Glasgow, that she realised the centre of governance was a better place to be than out on a limb. In London, there were greater opportunities to make things happen.

Not that the move was smooth sailing, she had effectively made herself homeless and put herself out of work; she could not work for her father, and her union role had been confined to Scotland. She fell on the mercy of her good friend Margaret in Gower Street in London, where they shared Margaret's flat for some months, until Mary had managed to establish herself in the capital.

Initially she sought work at a bookkeepers, but Margaret used her influence and networking skills to introduce Mary, to Lady Emilia Dilke and her niece Gertrude Tuckwell, this proved to be most fortuitous for Mary, as the Union that Lady Emilia was president of (and Gertrude Honorary Secretary for), the Women's Trade Unions League, were in the process of seeking a replacement for the much-treasured, and long-serving, Secretary

Mona Wilson. Mary was hastily interviewed, by these ladies and the Treasurer – David Shackleton – and offered the appointment. It is probably fair to say, with some trepidation, that although Mary was still very young at twenty-three, with little experience; what she lacked in experience she soon made up for with enthusiasm.

Mary re-organised the Union quickly, she was not one to accept disorder and found that the old regime under Mona was not to her standard, something that must have left Miss Wilson rather upset during the hand-over period. Mary realised quickly that the Union was sorely lacking in members, it had previously relied on male unions to affiliate their female members; there had been very little in the way of active recruitment. She went to work immediately, quite literally standing on a chair, or a box, outside factory gates encouraging women that it was in their best interests to join the union. She may not have yet become a polished public speaker, in the more official forum, but as a unionist to the women she served she was magnetic. It was noted that she did make mistakes in the early days, encouraging women that she would see that their wages went up by being in a union, of course when it had not happened in a week, she was practically mobbed outside one factory, but Mary learnt quickly, to promise only that which she could deliver.

In that first year, Lady Dilke took her under her wing, to smooth a few of the edges and make her into a more effective operator. As I have stressed in the last chapter – despite histories re-writing – both Gertrude Tuckwell and Lady Dilke, had built up considerable experience between them, Mary was very much the new-comer. She learnt the skill of negotiations in official meetings, and she refined her writing of effective prose to market the organisation to the members; this is illustrated most effectively in 'The Bundle of Sticks' which she wrote for the union journal – The Women Worker 1907, and I have included part of this article at the beginning of this book.

That first year taught Mary a great deal, and she was going to need it, unfortunately, in 1904 Lady Emilia died suddenly after a short illness, leaving her husband the MP – Sir Charles Dilke quite bereft. Mary was profoundly effected by the loss of her mentor, but even more determined that she must carry on the work in her honour, Gertrude assumed the role as president. By 1905 having increased membership substantially Mary found herself more and more, in the role having to settle disputes. She was constantly frustrated by the same problem, only in those factories where she could organise the women effectively could the pressure be applied to employers to increase the wages; however, there were still many more factories where only a few women would organise, there the union had no power and the wages would remain criminally low.

Although she had by now travelled extensively around the British Isles adding members and settling disagreements – working in London she had witnessed the worst of poverty. She saw first hand the deplorable, insanitary conditions that women were forced to work in; and as a consequence of their starvation wages, the poverty that they were reduced to living in, it made her angry. She met other activists such as Julia Varley, who insisted that only by organising women in the same union as men could things change, but Mary stuck to her beliefs that women needed to be organised separately. In her opinion, it was not just a case of giving women individual attention and support, it was more a case of very few male trade unions accepting women as members. The prevailing fear being that if they accepted women into a male trade union, then their wage would have to be equal to that of their male colleagues, something that the unions (and few in society) thought absolutely against the grain.

Mary was finding the WTUL to be too unwieldy, too large and out of touch with the grass-roots that she was interacting with. The other big problem with the union was, that if there were any large industrial actions they would never amount to anything, as the WTUL did not possess the funds that the male unions had (or were insured for) to enable them to withstand a big lock-out, Mary was painfully confronted with this when trying to assist the Dundee Jute workers. She knew there had to be a more locally-based union, that focused on the area's specific needs. In 1905 she managed to get the WTUL to consent to the forming of the National Federation of Women Workers, which was effectively an offshoot of the mother organisation, which shared the same offices and the same staff, she became president, and immediately set about the business of vast recruitment. This Federation had the focus of those women who were to be considered skilled or semi-skilled, yet were not of a professional level to be organised, all were on very meagre incomes and would take considerable persuasion of the value of parting with their hard-earned money, in order to pay union dues to receive greater protection. To overcome this, either she would have had to have used her own magnetic charm to recruit in-person – but as soon as she had left the numbers would start to decline – or she placed area organisers on the ground to work day-to-day. Julia Varley, an active trade unionist, ex-suffragette, was the woman chosen to take the Birmingham and Black Country area.

Her concept proved to be an effective one, by the end of 1906 the NFWW was boasting 2,000 members over 17 branches (Hamilton 1925). Initially employers treated this with derision and mockery, as did the fellow male trade unions, until the first disputes were settled in the union's favour. Mary had a simple strategy, every dispute was weighed up and considered, she would never enter any negotiations unless she knew that had a high chance of success (that is not to say that they were successful every time). She said that she would never support a strike action that she could not win. The theory was that if she put such efforts into any action which went against the Federation that it would destroy the Federations image and credibility. Mary understood the importance of success breeding success, and only being as good as your last success.

This bred in her a need to work with those of the lowest ranks of society. Mary witnessed many women having to survive on or below subsistence wages, many supporting families. This was a problem that had been well documented by others, particularly by those that Mary now worked with. She was also involved in the circle of those who were agitating for change on the national political stage. Sir Charles Dilke, had for a considerable time, pushed for Wages Boards to be set up to investigate the plight of the impoverished, particularly homeworkers. The homeworkers were by far the most poverty stricken, unions were unable to organise them because they were isolated and controlled by middlemen and women, who effectively enslaved them. This had been a cause that he had spent much effort investigating, first with Lady Emilia and then after her death. As I have explained in chapter 1, the pace of political change although moving was not quite ready to address these thorny issues just yet, more had to be highlighted in the public consciousness, to bring pressure to bear.

It is easy to speculate that as Mary, met the right people at the right time, and things appeared to have happened as a consequence, and that was somehow due to her, direct involvement, presence, or even her ideas that caused the tipping point. I believe that is far too simplistic an analysis, and one that has evolved from sympathetic biography. She was in the right place at the right time, but more importantly, she was associating with one of the most influential networks for social change. However, there is no doubt she was a catalyst and a dynamic force which became the public face. Most importantly, Mary was a modern young woman who understood the power of the newspapers, she knew how to operate the media and develop image, these skills were going to prove vitally important.

It was considered by this group of social radicals; Gertrude Tuckwell, David Shackleton, Sir Charles Dilke, J. J. Mallon, Will Anderson and Mary

Macarthur, that public humiliation of the government was needed to activate a groundswell of opinion to force them into action. The idea they chose to lead with was not a new one, it had been done in Berlin the previous year, but it was an effective strategy. They staged an Exhibition of Sweated Trades at the Queens Hall in London in 1906. This was supported by the funds primarily of George Cadbury, who was the proprietor of The Daily News; the editor – A. G. Gardiner, being part of Mary's network. This exhibition highlighted all that was vile in the exploitative society that the Edwardians were profiting from. Probably it was Mary – as she had made contact with many by now – who assembled the vast collection of workers from; cardboard box-makers, shirt-makers, button makers, button-card threaders, lace-makers, and many others, including chainmakers. The exhibition ran from the 2nd to the 29th May and thousands witnessed, the hard labours, over long hours, for little money, that these people were subjected to.

It caused the public outcry that was necessary, the organisers were quick to act to capitalise on this and keep the public momentum whipped up. The National Anti-Sweating League was formed, of which Mary was a founding member. This was all that Sir Charles, and the likes of Winston Churchill needed, to force the setting up of the Select Committee to hear evidence on Homework. Many were to be called before that committee, Mary being one of the people who would give most time making representation on behalf of the many workers that she now represented. Her tireless dynamism, meant that she pushed herself harder and longer than most, often putting herself in personal danger in order to collect research, this selflessness was brought home to committee, when Mary contracted Diphtheria.

She had been visiting girls who made baby clothes in their homes, and then sold them on through middlemen for a pittance. She had met with one such young girl, in the East End living in appalling conditions; she did not even possess any blankets to cover herself with at night, and used the baby clothes instead. Mary bought some of the baby clothes as evidence for the committee, and fell sick before she was to make the presentation, she was diagnosed with Diphtheria, probably contracted from the baby clothes themselves. This horrified the Select Committee, who were shocked that their own families could be put at such risks to their health, through the inhumanity shown to sweated workers.

As I have explained previously, the plight of the chainmakers was not a new thing, it had been known about and investigated previously, and it is likely that the WTUL were instrumental in bringing a chainmaker to give her account, along with the lace-maker, and a shirt-maker, and a box maker. The weight of evidence was so compelling, that Winston Churchill was able to bring a Bill before the House in 1909, which passed into law at the beginning of 1910. This Act established four Trade Boards in the occupations highlighted above, who were to investigate and agree on a minimum wage in each area. As is often said, the battle was won, but the war was far from over, and probably many, Mary in particular, realised that it would take more to give the tiger teeth.

At this point I am going to move away from the actions of 1910 and the Chainmakers' strike itself, as the penultimate chapters are devoted to the happenings and the outcomes of the actions taken. Suffice to say, this book would not be written had it not been successful, I believe that it is more important to focus on the remainder of Mary's life to enable her history to be contextualised, and remove some of the mythologizing which is ever-present.

The Cradley dispute was either the watershed, or the catalyst for the time we now call the 'Great Unrest'. There is no doubt that the publically applauded success of that action, led to a whole host of industrial actions that caught like wildfire. For the first time in industrial history, the exploited workers realised that they had a voice, that would be listened to, and most importantly, that public opinion was on their side to make a change to their lives.

Mary found herself, not only having to channel all of her energies into the continuation of the Trade Board's process in the other three scheduled trades, but deal with ever-more increasing industrial unrest. Within the three years leading up to the Great War, she was stretched in all directions, physically and mentally. She finally agreed to marry Will Anderson, and within a short time thereafter, persuaded him to agree to moving next to the Federation offices in Mecklenborough Square; so that she could continue to work, making sure each of the minimum wage agreements were made and applied.

At that time, the infant Health Insurance Bill was making its progress through the House. Mary knew that this Bill, more than any other, could have a profound positive and negative impact on the women she served. Being the poorest of people, they were the ones to suffer greatest ill-health and by the fact of being the home-makers and child-bearers, they were the ones who would benefit the most from the support given. But, the government was insisting on a contributory scheme, of which she was opposed, as these women had very little spare income. She managed to reach a compromise, where only those above a certain income would pay a due, and set up a scheme through the Federation to challenge the expensive Post Office alternative.

There followed the intense lobbying for the Health Insurance Bill combined with additional pressures of the Bermondsey strike – where most of the East End; jam-making, confectionery and glue factories came out on wild cat strikes – leaving Mary having to settle twenty plus disputes, and organise strikers' support through donations of food. All of this frenzied activity brought huge tolls on her personal health. In 1913 she lost the baby boy that she had been carrying, and realised that she had to slow down. But fate intervened once more with the outbreak of war the following year, a time when both Will and Mary found themselves on the wrong side of public opinion, as pacifists, both favouring a negotiated peace.

When the war finally came, it had to be accepted as an inevitability and got on with, something which Mary did always with an eye to how this war might affect those that she had fought so hard for. When the high wave of unemployment that was caused forced many of her women out of work, she immediately acted to help Queen Mary, establish her 'Queen's Work For Women Fund.' She worked meticulously to ensure that factory regulations were applied, and no undercutting of prices were given in order to ensure the payment of living wages.

The following year she delivered a healthy baby girl, Nancy, and simultaneously fought against 'dilution' of women in war work, rather than 'substitution'. She was acutely aware, that although by now there was an acute labour shortage and the inflationary costs of persecuting a war combining with the ever-increasing cost of living, as a consequence, wages were deflating. On more than one occasion she confronted Lloyd George, first when he was Chancellor of the Exchequer and then when he became Minister of Munitions (following the Shell Crisis), to push the government into action to increase women's wages to meet with inflation.

The end of the war, brought more unrest which Mary was in the forefront of having to manage, when the government forced all their munitions workers (mainly women) out of work immediately, with no income. Mary headed off the unofficial march on the Embankment, of Woolwich Arsenal workers headed for Whitehall, furious at their ill-treatment. Once again, Mary used her influential, rapid-negotiation techniques, to allow the illegal protest to complete the route without coming under fire from the local militia (it was illegal to march down Whitehall whilst the House was in session), and with her persuasive charm negotiated urgent intermediate payments.

Lloyd George was determined to capitalise on the euphoria and jingoism of a hard-won war, and had called a rapid election to secure his mandate from the people to continue. The election planned for December, called for Will to campaign in his constituency in Sheffield, at the same time Mary had decided to stand as candidate in Stourbridge. This ward was the patch where Mary had carved out the famous Cradley Heath victory, and should have worked in her favour, but for four issues. Firstly, only half of the constituency were the poor and under-privileged who revered her as 'Our Mary' but possessing extremely low levels of literacy. Secondly, Lloyd George had been none too impressed with the intervention of 'Miss Macarthur' in recent years, and had decided to give his coupon to another candidate standing. Thirdly; her pacifist leanings and that of her husband's were used as political capital against her, she was accused of having pro-German sympathies, an allegation that she vehemently denied. The final blow which sealed her fate, was that the electoral officials refused to accept her standing in her maiden name and insisted that she stand as Mrs Mary Anderson, a name which she had never used, and certainly one that she was not known by. The simple folk who knew her as Mary Macarthur, were already in a state of confusion, many only having received the right to vote for the first time, most were illiterate, and many ballot papers would have been incorrectly filled as she was unknown by that name.

Will's campaign was equally ruthless, and when his defeat was announced her first act was to telegram him immediately and tell him that 'it is better to be right than first'. In her post-election address she pointedly remarked, 'who steals my purse steals trash, but he who filches my good name etc...' Both were exhausted and quite deflated by the Christmas of 1918, and in between the election run-up and the results on the 28th December spent their time with their daughter. After that Christmas they attempted to return life to normal, Mary back to the Federation, Will once again back out on the campaign trail.

However, this was the year of the Spanish Flu, sadly in the February Nancy contracted the virus, while Will was away. Nancy was young and able to come through, when Will returned it was clear he too had contracted it, but he had breathing complications. Mary and her friends maintained a bedside vigil, day and night with him, but on the 25th February 1919 Will Anderson died.

It is written that Mary was never herself afterwards, that she had lost her soul mate and was too grief stricken to continue her dynamic approach to living, it is certainly true that year she wrote very negatively about life, but she did continue to actively work, even taking on new challenges. She made two trips for Peace Conferences to America, and she took on the mantle of fighting for a criminal justice system that would offer legal aid to the poor.

Mary was told some time later that year, or in early 1920, that she had stomach cancer, a shock for everyone that she confided in. But even that did not stop her relentless efforts. Her final battle was to wind up the NFWW, thanks to her successful negotiations over the years with the male trade unions (particularly the most resistant of those the engineering unions). Mary had fought long and hard for the unions to accept women into their organisations, her final convincing arguments had been much helped by the war. She had on numerous occasions pointed out that if the employers managed to exploit new machinery, or women workers, they could effectively put men out of work, or pay them less, and that only by standing shoulder to shoulder could the unions take on the employers and win.

After a couple of unsuccessful operations and treatments, Mary lost her biggest fight on New Years Day 1921. More or less at the same time, the NFWW ceased to exist and had become amalgamated to the General Workers' Union.

Obviously, Mary's untimely death, so close to the tragedy of losing her husband – who had been tipped for bigger things in the ILP – shaped much of what was written, by many who knew her and worked with her personally. Understandably, the shock of the calamity which had befallen her was too much for many and it showed in their eulogies. This is not to dismiss any of Mary's significant works or achievements, which would make most heads spin, merely to add a note of caution that this was a time when many actively worked for social change, Mary was one. There is no doubt, that she had more energies than most, and she knew the importance of the media to her role, and thanks to those around her she learnt how to be a skilled negotiator and a crafted speaker. She had a gift to inspire and lead, and those things would be what was most needed when the biggest dispute of her life was faced; the one she knew that she had to win.

Chapter 7

BY THE SWEAT OF THEIR BROW

"The sweating evil has long engaged the attention of social and industrial workers in many fields. Some have approached it from the philanthropic point of view, and have sought a remedy in voluntary means such as consumers' leagues; others have approached it from the point of view of industrial organisation, and have sought to deal with it by the extension of trade unionism and legislative action. So far all efforts alike have been futile. The evil is too widespread and too remote in its operations to be touched by charity. It involves a class too forlorn, too isolated, and too impoverished to be reached by trade unionism. The cry of the victims has hitherto been too feeble and hopeless to command the attention of Parliament."

(Black 1907)

This was the introduction written by A. G. Gardiner to Clementina Black's book which was published in 1907, entitled 'Sweated Industry'. It was written just after the London Exhibition, which frames most of this chapter, and just before any legislation was enacted to counteract what Gardiner rightly termed as 'the sweating evil'. Many of the people featured in this book had been provoked to take action against the effects of sweating, in order to do so, a few researched the subject widely to try to ascertain possible causes, in order to find solutions.

Here I will endeavour to outline these identified causes, and how some remedies were more effective than others, culminating in 'The Daily News Exhibition of Sweated Industries', and the subsequent formation of the National Anti-Sweating League. All of which placed the crisis of exploitation into the public consciousness and highlighted particular areas of employment for radical change, particularly the chainmakers of Cradley Heath.

As with much that I have already written, it must be read in the temporal context. British society was still very fixed in the strongly held moralities of Victorianism. Some comments ascribed to socialist thinkers of the day, may appear privileged, even racist, I do not hold with these views, but I accept that it was the underlying moral discourse of the time, that led to judgemental generalisation of the ethics and morals of those affected by some who were in a position of far greater privilege.

Charles Booth, Mr and Mrs Sidney Webb and Seebohm Rowntree, had led the first wave of publication that shocked all who read their works. Obviously, these books were written from three very different perspectives although they shared some common beliefs. Charles Booth had a strong desire towards temperance, and considered many of the ills of society lay with alcohol. The Webbs were the first couple that were considered as dedicated social researchers, taking a far more pragmatic approach to observing the lives of the underclass. Seebohm Rowntree, like Edward Cadbury later, had business interests combined with religious belief that focussed him to examine the problems from a more philanthropic perspective, ultimately with a view to improving the working conditions of their staff and in turn increase productivity.

These works provoked an explosion of studies and annual reports from various inspectorates of factories, and organisations, who were adamant in their collective opinions that something must be done. Perhaps the most circulated – and because of the connections to Lloyd George and the Liberal party – the most vocal, was The Daily News with A. G. Gardiner at the helm, and George Cadbury as the proprietor. This paper was more able to reach the masses and arrive on the breakfast table in a confrontational mode, than the books and tracts that were circulated through those that had an interest in the first place. It would be The Daily News that would spearhead the vanguard to bring these problems to the public's attention in a manner that could no longer be ignored.

Although I have already discussed this in a different context in chapter 4, I feel it is important to remind ourselves of what exactly was 'sweating' and why had it had existed; most importantly, why had it become so prevalent in the new industrial society. Clementina Black (1907) describes sweating thus:

"The term 'sweating', to which at one time the notion of sub-contract was attached, has gradually come to be applied to almost any method of work under which workers are extremely ill-paid or extremely over-worked; and the 'sweater' means nowadays 'the employer who cuts down wages below the level of decent subsistence, works his operatives for excessive hours, or compels them to toil under insanitary conditions'."

Sweating was not new, in fact, it had existed as long as things had been produced, and cheaper labour could undercut others, and as handcraft moved over to more mechanised modes of production, sweating began to proliferate, as a consequence. Some operations simply did not lend themselves to the investment in expensive plant and equipment, or there was not the desire or necessity to invent machinery to effect the task. Some processes were simply too labour intensive and could not be broken down into mechanized operations. Or the product end-cost would be too prohibitive, if the capital investment were to be made in machinery, thus, pairs of hands were cheaper. Added to this, if all these products had become factory-based, that would mean more people to watch over, and although wages were not particularly good, more people to pay. For the employer what they did not see, they did not have to bother themselves about, as long as the job was done, the product made and sold for a healthy profit that was all that was considered important. Cadbury and Shann (1907) placed this need of the employer to distance himself from outwork and dependence on the middlemen, in these terms:

> "Moreover, as pointed out above, the payment of low wages is often the line of least resistance when an unscrupulous employer wishes to reduce his cost of production, and when cheapness of cost is prevented on the lines of low wages the trade is bound to fall back on some other method, such as improved machinery or more efficient management. And though this maybe less immediately profitable, in the long run it is more advantageous than the old method of subsidised labour. The necessity of such improved methods would in most cases give the advantage to the larger employers and thus small masters would be driven from the trade, but this would be an economic advantage for the community as a whole. At the present time many small masters continue to exist just because they are enabled to compete with the more efficient factories by paying miserable wages to their sweated women. It would be an almost unqualified gain to drive all such trades as box-making, paper bag-making, etc., into factories where machines could do the work. It is altogether uneconomic for women to compete with machinery that can do the work so much more expeditiously that the sweated worker can."

Sweating had long proliferated in the trades of tailoring and shirt making, these were skilled operations that were too expensive to mechanize. Much of this employment was London-based and emanated from the best tailors in London many of whom were Jewish, this led to a raft of anti-Semitist commentators who saw the proliferation of sweating as rooted in race. Unfortunately, the Fabians and their supporters were of like-mind in condemning a race that they perceived as being central to the mass causes of exploitation, (Hutchins 1908):

Fig. 1. Mary Reid Macarthur
(courtesy of James Deane – grandson of M. R. Macarthur).

Fig. 2. Sir Charles Dilke MP.

Fig. 3. George Cadbury, 1839 – 1922.
Philanthropist and founder of Bournville Garden City for factory workers,
and proprietor of the Daily News.

Fig. 4. Woman chainmaker in Cradley Heath. With grateful thanks to the TUC Library Collections, London Metropolitan University.

Fig. 5. A group of girls working in a backstreet forge in Cradley Heath. With grateful thanks to the TUC Library Collections, London Metropolitan University.

Fig. 6. A picture of NFWW women 1908. Julia Varley, unknown woman, Mary Macarthur (seated) and Jessie Stephens. With grateful thanks to the TUC Library Collections, London Metropolitan University.

Fig. 7. Mary Macarthur and Kier Hardie taking tea.
With grateful thanks to the Trustees of the National Library of Scotland.

Fig. 8. Kier Hardie and Mary Macarthur. Courtesy of the Press Association.

Fig. 9. Mary Macarthur leading a rally in Cradley Heath, High Street. Photograph reproduced with the kind permission of the Black Country Living Museum.

Fig. 10. Crowd of supporters and family outside the Empire Theatre in Cradley Heath. Photograph reproduced with the kind permission of the Black Country Living Museum.

Fig. 11. Strikers with Julia Varley (to the front middle) and Patience Round (to her right). Photograph reproduced with the kind permission of the Black Country Living Museum.

Fig. 12. Mary Macarthur rallying the crowd. Photograph reproduced with the kind permission of the Black Country Living Museum.

Fig. 13. Thomas Sitch. Photograph reproduced with the kind permission of the Black Country Living Museum.

Fig. 14. Votes for women. Punch cartoon. 1910.

KING COPHETUA AND THE BEGGAR-MAID.

The King (Mr. Asquith). "'THIS BEGGAR-MAID SHALL BE MY QUEEN'—THAT IS, IF THERE'S A GENERAL FEELING IN THE COUNTRY TO THAT EFFECT."

Fig. 15. Asquith and female suffrage. Punch cartoon. 1908.

THE WAR WORKERS.

"WHAT'S ALL THIS CACKLE ABOUT VOTES AND A NEW REGISTER?"
"DON'T KNOW—OR CARE. WE'RE ALL TOO BUSY JUST NOW."

Fig. 16. Munitions. Punch cartoon. 1916.

Fig. 17. Chainmakers' Festival 2009.

Fig. 18. Chainmakers' Festival 2009.

Fig. 19. Chainmakers' Festival 2009.

Fig. 20. Chainmakers' Festival. 2009.

"The evil effect of the Jew's competition lies in the characteristics which render him a fit subject for the pestilential conditions of home work; he over-crowds whole districts; his standards of comfort are low; and his ingenuity has created or organized new industries to suit the circumstances."

This flagrant racism on behalf of the Fabians was also used against the myriad of unskilled labour-intensive tasks that were put out to sweating, such as; match box making, card box making, button carding, hook and eye carding, to name but a few. It seems that it was easier to castigate blame on one offending group in society (whom it was fashionable at that time to blame for all the moral ills) than to admit that there might be many others from their own race responsible for the creation of the 'evil'. The author had to concur that there was no evidence of 'foreigners' in the chainmaking sector, yet sweating was happening on a grand scale.

In the 'Handbook for the Sweated Industries Exhibition in London' in 1906, which was produced by The Daily News and edited by Richard Mudie-Smith, some anti-Semitic references are made by a very unusual source – Mr and Mrs Ramsay MacDonald; they were both high-profile members of The Fabian Society. The handbook itself was produced for the exhibition that was staged for the whole of May at The Queen's Hall. George Cadbury was the major financial benefactor, but it was a coming together of many of the names featured in this book that made the exhibition the startling reality it became.

The council for the exhibition itself was made up of fifty-nine members, with the Rev. Professor George Adam Smith as President and Alfred G. Gardiner in the Chair. Thirty-two of the council members sat as executive, it is interesting to note that at this stage neither George or Edward Cadbury did so, they merely participated as council members. Clementina Black, Mary Macarthur, Margaret MacDonald, George Shann and Gertrude Tuckwell all sat on the executive. Three other notable names appear of the list of council members for the exhibition; George Bernard Shaw, H. G. Wells and Keir Hardie.

Richard Mudie-Smith was secretary to the council and charged with the organisation of the exhibition, which lasted the whole month, with daily contributions of lectures from those I have listed and many others including, B. L. Hutchins (Elizabeth) and Ramsay MacDonald himself. In Clementina Black's book from the following year on 'Sweated Industries', Gardiner in his introduction enlightens us further as to how these lectures were received and the same question that was continually posed to each speaker, (Black 1907):

" "Isn't the remedy Protection?" was a question frequently heard at the lectures given at the Exhibition. Most of us would agree with Mr Bernard Shaw who, in answering such a question, said he would be ready to protect our industry against sweated competition. But generally operation of Protection would be wholly in the interest of the sweater. It would put a new premium upon his vocation. And the fact remains that sweating is more rampant in protected countries even than our own."

This issue of protection versus free-trade had split the Liberals with Joseph Chamberlain leading the split-away faction, causing the Liberals to lose power for twenty years. Subsequently, this act then lost Balfour the 1906 general election, due to collapse of the alliance with the Liberal unionists. It was very much part and parcel of the economic discourse of the time, and something that was feared by many as being divisive and damaging.

The catalogue opens with a description of the Berlin Exhibition which had taken place in the January of that year and stimulated the German government to action from the combined pressure of the German public and the Empress herself. It was hoped that the exhibition which was to be staged in London on a much grander scale would have the same effect on those that could make a difference. The winds were set fair for strong support as the General Election of January/February of that year had returned the Liberals led by Campbell-Bannerman with a large majority, with 29 Labour MPs led by Keir Hardie. Mudie-Smith was careful in his introductory notes not at this stage to criticise the employers directly for the present state of affairs, but rather indirectly by highlighting the commercial system of competitiveness as being at fault, he writes:

"Sweating follows unrestricted competition as naturally and inevitably as pain follows disease."

In the preface written by Gertrude Tuckwell, she quotes Beatrice Webb when she describes how everyone is culpable in what they are about to witness at the exhibition, she writes with force:

"'The sweater', says Mrs Sydney Webb, 'is the whole nation, for employer, shopkeeper, and purchaser all contribute to create and keep alive the system I have described, and our guilt is not only that which attaches to passive tolerance by us as citizens of any wrong or suffering in the state, but amounts to active, if ignorant, participation in oppression'."

Clementina Black then offers remedies to the four evils that she has identified from sweating; excessive hours; unsuitability of the work-place; the employment of child labour and low pay. Among the restriction of free competition and various acts of legislation to inhibit long hours, bad conditions and child labour, she advocates the establishment of a Consumer's League to promote the purchase of goods from verified producers. She subsequently made a similar recommendation in her own book. A scheme that she acknowledges has been successful in New York yet already failed in England, for the counter reason that the New York scheme had succeeded. Whereas in New York they had attracted supporters from wealth and celebrity, in England they had failed to attract anyone of notoriety or substance. It was in all probability her advocacy of the establishment of a minimum wage over the strongly held opinion of the Women Industrial Council for a Consumer League, that would eventually lead to Black's divergence of opinion with Margaret MacDonald.

One of the most important entries in the handbook is one drawing the reader's attention to the Wages Board Bill proposed by Sir Charles Dilke. A Bill that everyone feared would fail to become law in present session as not enough time was available in the House for discussion. The Bill was described as a 'good answer' for the present problem, as through its adoption Wages Boards could be established to assess the correct payment of what might be a minimum wage for a particular occupation; the sum could be specified and then payment enforced.

The exhibition comprised of twenty-four stalls, with forty-five workers. The trades exhibited were; trouser making, cabinet making, matchbox making, hook and eye carding, buttons carding, tennis ball sewing, racquet ball covering, slipper making, making children's boot uppers, making men's umbrellas, covering sunshades, making grummets (grommets), sack making, making baby's bonnets, tie making, brush drawing, fur sewing, vamp beading (ladies' shoes), beading ornaments, blouse making, shawl fringing, making children's knicker-bockers, belt making, military embroidery, hosiery making, glove stitching, making confirmation wreaths, making pinafores, cigarette case making, pipe and cigarette-holder making, chemise making, making ladies' fancy aprons and shirt making. Mudie-Smith was at pains to note that no payment was to be offered to those working, and they had been instructed to accept none from the visitors.

There was also a vast range of exhibits from many sweated trades catalogued for the visitors to inspect, four hundred and forty-three to be precise. Including oddities such as; bodice steels, pom-poms, dolls heads, mouse-traps, tin cucumber slicers and coffin tassels. In this carefully compiled list alongside each entry there is the rate paid and the average hours worked, with any additional remarks. Chainmaking appears here, and is listed as 5/- per cwt, averaging twelve hours worked, and with the additional comment that women had to make 2 cwt per week, and out of their earnings pay 3/- for fuel.

The handbook also contains over forty descriptive entries of the lives and work of the various sweated workers. George Shann supplied three of these entries; the Birmingham hook and eye carders, button carders of Birmingham, and chainmaking from Cradley Heath and district. In these he describes how the women in Birmingham had their whole families threading cards with fiddly hooks and eyes for a pittance, the smaller deft fingers of their children being put to good use, but with a price to pay, children unclean, a house unclean through lack of time and lost childhoods. He describes the young fourteen year old girls having to start in chainmaking and being tied for the rest of their lives to the forge. Then marrying and having to mind their children while they worked. He also accredits the blame of the lack of mechanization in the trade due to the 'cheapness of the women's work'.

Clementina Black contributed towards racquet and tennis ball covering, she draws the reader's attention to the arduous labour to produce a gross of racquet balls for 2/- that will subsequently sell for 21/-. Margaret Irwin made an entry of shawl fringing, where she emphasised that the decreasing price in the garments had led to serious cuts in earnings for the women; now making 9/- per week when four years previously they had been able to earn 17/-. The whole catalogue gives a comprehensive view of the lives of the sweated worker, one stands out for me more than most. It is an anecdotal story provided by George Haw at the end of part one of the catalogue, and is entitled 'The Home-life of the Sweated'. Like Rebecca's Story, I have included this within the appendices of this book.

L. G. Chiozza Money MP, who had contributed towards Sir Charles Dilke's Wages Board Bill, makes an excellent entry on match box making. In this he describes the monotonous assemblage of box after box to earn a pittance, a woman with a child making eight gross in a week (1152 boxes), and possibly earning 8/-. But he then draws our attention to a campaign which had been run in the previous year by The Daily News to contact manufacturers directly to establish if they knew how and where these boxes were being made, and nail manufacturers who would use the boxes. One such enquiry ended up on the manager's desk at Kynoch's in Birmingham, the reply that came is printed in the handbook:

TO THE EDITOR OF THE DAILY NEWS

"Sir, – Our attention has been drawn to the remarks under the above heading in your issues of the 24th and 30th of November, in regard to tack-boxes purchased by Hadley & Shorthouse, Limited, Mitre Works Birmingham.

"Hadley and Shorthouse, Limited, is a Kynoch company, and were buying the boxes from Messrs. J. Deaton & Sons, Usher Road, Old Ford, London, who they believed were the manufacturers.

"We have written Messer. Deaton, inviting their remarks, and in the meantime have pleasure in enclosing our cheque value one guinea as a contribution towards the relief of the family who, it appears, were working under such distressing conditions.

Yours faithfully, for Kynoch Limited

"Frank Huxham,

"Secretary and Manager."

It is not hard to see how many manufacturers in the provinces may have been fooled into believing that their packaging was fairly made, or they just chose not to find out. However, with the chainmakers this exploitation is a very different story, of local employers and manufacturers only too aware of the prevailing conditions in which the women were expected to work and quite happy to accept the status quo, for they blamed the problems squarely on the shoulders of the women themselves. The women had to work out of economic necessity, yet women had no protection or rights to representation. The male unions refused to allow them to join, the argument that was given time after time to the male members was that the women were undercutting their wages. Yet, many of the male workers were married to women chainmakers and expected them to continue working, for without their wage the families found it impossible to survive. However, for the employer with recessionary markets and wealth of available cheap workers, they could afford to keep the exploitation thriving for their profits.

The Exhibition was opened by Princess Henry of Battenberg and held to huge acclaim, Gardiner acknowledges the newspaper's triumph (Black 1907):

"The exhibition held right in the heart of West London, visited by thirty-thousand people, and commanding the attention of all serious students of our social system, brought the question instantly into the sphere of practical politics. Sweating was no longer a vague term concerning some or more apocryphal wrongs. It was made real and actual."

And he continues a few pages later:

"The profound impression made by the Exhibition found expression in a universal desire for action. The question one heard again and again was 'What can we do? What can we do?' It was a question that the Princess of Wales asked as she passed round the stalls where the workers were engaged at their various forms of slavery. It was the question that continued like a hopeless refrain throughout the six weeks of the Exhibition. Most people came with vague ideas of the evil and went away with vaguer ideas of the remedy. Many of them were doubtless glad to forget this contact with that other forlorn world which seemed such a disquieting challenge to the splendour and luxury of the world of society. It was a painful interlude between a visit to the shops in the morning and a visit to the theatre in the evening.

The general feeling however was not one of idle curiosity, but of grave concern, and when the Exhibition closed it was felt that the public conscience once awakened must not be allowed to go to sleep again."

The stage was set, the general public had been shocked into ardent and vocal support, now there had to be a campaign of applied pressure from all those 'great and good' to the seat of Government itself. Later that year the National Anti-Sweating League was convened, with George Cadbury as President and a most notable list of Vice Presidents including; Sir Charles Dilke MP, Lord Dunraven, Rt. Hon. Herbert Gladstone, Mr J. C. Gray, Mr Keir Hardie MP, Canon Scott Holland, Miss Irwin, Earl of Lytton, Rev. J. Scott Lidgett, Mr William Maxwell, The Chief Rabbi: Mr W. Pember Reeves, Bishop of Ripon, Mr and Mrs Sydney Webb, Mr H. G. Wells, Mr Henry Vivian. The honorary treasurer was the Earl of Beauchamp and the honorary secretary was George Shann. The executive committee was chaired by Alfred G. Gardiner and included in the list once again were; Clementina Black, Mary Macarthur and Gertrude Tuckwell. At sometime in the following year or so J. J. Mallon assumed the role of honorary secretary.

Their immediate response was to convene a conference lasting three days at The Guildhall in London. The conference was opened by the Lord Mayor and was said to represent two million organised workers. The remit of the newly formed league was to secure the minimum wage and as such stressed the need to support the Wages Boards Bill which was once again before Parliament. Sir Charles Dilke, Clementina Black and Sydney Webb were among those who gave addresses to the conference, to raise the spectre of sweating once more, and propose the setting of a minimum wage.

By 1908 the leadership of the Liberal party was forced to change as Campbell-Bannerman had to resign on grounds of ill health. Herbert

Asquith assumed the role of Prime Minister, he was known for his strong opposition to women's suffrage, but David Lloyd George was the counter-balance to that view in the cabinet and could be seen to turn the opinions of Asquith. The NASL decided that it was time to make another show of strength and make their presence felt, so that the campaign for the minimum wage would not be engulfed in the interregnum.

The Times of December 1908 reports of the deputation that visited number 10, it gives the entire list of the names who presented themselves before the Prime Minister that day, the impact must have been startling as much as it is to read now. The list commences with The Archbishop of Canterbury, the Bishop of Ripon, The Bishop of Birmingham, Archbishop Bourne, Father Bernard Vaughan, Dr Cliff, Dr Horton, Rev. J. Scott Lidgett, the Rev. Sylvester Horne, the Chief Rabbi, Lord Milner, Lord Dunraven, Lord Lytton, Sir Charles Dilke MP, Sir Thomas Whittaker MP, George Toulmin MP, Mr L. G. C. Money MP, Mr J. W. Hills MP, Mr W. C. Bridgeman MP, Mr Kier Hardie MP, Mr D. Shackleton MP, Mr Arthur Henderson MP, Mr J. R. Clynes MP, Mr F. Richards MP, Mr J. O'Grady MP, Mr Charles Fenwick MP, Mr H. J. Tennant MP, Mrs Herbert Gladstone (representing the Industrial Law Committee), Miss Gertrude Tuckwell (chairman), Miss Mary Macarthur (secretary of WTUL), Miss Clementina Black, Miss Llewelyn Davies (Women's Cooperative Guild), Miss N. Adler (Wages Earning Children Committee), Mr and Mr Sydney Webb, Miss Lily Montague (girls clubs) Mrs Margaret Frain (Scottish Council for Women's Trades), Mr H. G. Wells, and Mr and Mrs Pember Reeves, Mr Thomas Holmes, Rev. H. Russell Wakefield, Mr Henry Vivian MP and Mr A. G. Gardiner.

Added to this long list of notables, many had sent letters of regret at being unable to attend, among those was Austen Chamberlain MP (the eldest son of Joseph). It is noted that Mr Asquith was sympathetic, I conclude in the light of the sheer weight of numbers and their positions of influence, he would have been a foolish Prime Minister indeed to ignore the entreaty. The following year Winston Churchill's Trade Boards Bill was passed into law, while it was making its stately progress through the various stages of reading, the NASL was applying the pressure with those public speakers of greatest effect, George Bernard Shaw gave one particularly memorable speech.

It is recorded in The Daily Chronicle, June 1909, that GBS was speaking out to a 'Society Audience' regarding the 'minimum wage'. George Bernard Shaw is quoted thus:

"I don't want to improve your minds, I don't care enough about them, I want to get something done."

And he is quoted further:

"A truth that has been reserved for me to discover, merely, that what the poor suffer from is poverty…Another simple fact, that had been waiting for me to explain, is that there is one way to relieve the poverty of the poor give them money."

One can only wonder at the faces of the assembled audience as he skewered them with his acerbic wit and ridicule, all taken in the right way of course he was GBS. His final quote must have left them rolling in the aisles:

"But it is the poor who object. They like being poor. There is something virtuous in being miserable. Here, for instance, are you rich folk paying to hear me speak on the minimum wage! I have repeatedly offered to address meetings of the poor on the same question for nothing, nay, I have stood at the street corner and harangued them unasked – but I find it difficult to get them to listen to me at all."

This constant pressure from the vanguard of the most notable in society was enough to propel the government to take action. Many years of hard work, of collective research and organisation had been necessary to bring all of the people and all of the agents for change comprehensively together at the right time. Mary Macarthur had been active throughout the first decade of the twentieth century in promoting these activities, she had become a strong and eloquent voice, she possessed the charisma to organise and there was a team of very capable and vastly experienced individuals behind her. She had given comprehensive evidence to the Select Committee into Homework, which I shall discuss in the ensuing chapter, and even contracted diphtheria in her endeavours to gather evidence. But all that struggle had paid off, finally there was an Act in place and the minimum wage looked as if it was now within everyone's grasp to achieve it, all that had to be done at that moment was to bring the various Trade Boards together to ascertain and set wages in the first four scheduled trades to come; card box making, shirt making, chainmaking and machine-made lace finishing. The first board to meet would be that for the chainmakers.

Chapter 8

THE TRADE OFF

The history of the chainmaking industry in the Black Country was one of exploitation and discontent. It had been the subject of a few reports and texts, noting the dreadful conditions and the poor pay of workers. There had been a number of significant strikes previously, which had mirrored the national economic situation of the country; when the economy was in depression, so the workers were facing ever-greater financial hardship and would organise to raise their case. But it was only ever the male workers that were in this position to push for change and they had access to trade union membership to promote their cause. The women continued to be the thorn in the side, to the male trade unions, who wished to be seen by their male members as being active just for them.

The union leaders portrayed the women not as victims, but as the cause of much of the male chain workers' bad pay and conditions. This to some extent was a fair analysis, the women worked in the domestic sphere of the industry, they had no rights in law and no access to representation. As a consequence, they were easily manipulated and isolated, and forced to work for less than their competitors; thus undermining the male domestic outworkers. The unions exploited this image, casting the women as stealing the work from under the men's noses; taking away a man's rights as the breadwinner. Sometimes this strategy had been effective, in creating division amongst the chain workers, but there were many men who were only too aware, that if their wives and daughters were not to work their incomes would be decimated, or those men who had been witness to the many widows who had to support themselves in some way; these reasons at times brought some degree of sympathy from the male members of the community.

Additionally, the employers tended to use mainly men in the factories for the much larger, heavier manual work, the gauge of chain that was produced there was of a substantial size. As more and more men gravitated towards the factory employment, there were more women employed to take the domestic outworking, at significantly lower rates than their male predecessors. The industry became divided between men earning higher rates in factories and women earning a pittance producing the small chain. For the unions this was an effective division of labour, making it far more straightforward to manage and organise their members, for the most part ignoring the female counterparts. Even as Barnsby (1998) notes when Thomas Sitch – who would be most influential in the dispute – appeared in Cradley Heath in 1894 and headed the Chainmakers' and Strikers' Union, still no consideration was given to the women, in fact:

"By 1896 the Chainmakers' & Strikers' Union were well able to look after the factory workers, but the plight of the domestic worker continued dire."

This was despite the fact that the UK was, at that point, emerging from the Great Depression of the 1880's, and economic prosperity was increasing. It was too easy for the 'foggers' to maintain their sharp practice and keep the women on starvation wages, simply because no union would trouble themselves with women workers. There was an attempt made by the WTUL under Lady Emilia Dilke, with the active support of Clementina Black in 1886 to get the women to organise, but they came up against considerable opposition from male trade unions in the Midlands, who viewed them as fighting a feminist battle and depriving the men of their rightful wage (Morgan 2001). The attempt foundered through lack of support from the other unions and the WTUL did not manage to recruit, or retain, more than twenty percent of the women to the union.

With the resurgence of the WTUL under Gertrude Tuckwell and Mary Macarthur, followed by the formation of the NFWW, the union became a focus of strength for women's organisation. With their subsequent involvement in the National Anti-Sweating League, and no doubt Macarthur's dynamic drive and determination, her attention was brought to the helplessness of the women workers of Cradley Heath. Thomas Sitch had also drawn very similar conclusions, that the fight for all chainmakers whether men or women, could only be won if they were united in that fight (Morgan 2001). However, there was a division of the labour force that had been achieved through the men becoming factory-based and the women replacing the domestic production. Added to this, there was a perception amongst many men, that they were the workers with greater rights, being the traditional breadwinners, this was a fine line to walk for Sitch and Macarthur. How did they enable the organisation of women, without antagonising the existing male unions?

The solution came with the formation of the Cradley Heath Women Chainmakers' Union by Thomas Sitch, aided by Mary Macarthur who came to the region to talk. There followed rapid enrolment into the union, and by June 1907, it was reported that 1,100 had been recruited with between 700 to 800 paying their dues of 2d per week (Morgan 2001). However, yet another economic depression had overcome the country. The price of chain fell, this was further accentuated by the British Navy making the decision to build larger and fewer ships, requiring much less chains of shorter length. The Black Country was yet again thrown into financial turmoil (Blackburn 1987). This had a detrimental affect on the new union's numbers – which by now had been renamed the Hand Hammered Branch of the NFWW – despite attempts to rally the numbers, by both Mary Macarthur and Julia Varley; as the recession bit in to already low wages, decisions had to be made whether to pay union dues or buy bread to feed a mouth.

The women's union continued to press their case that the advent of the new proposed legislation was the only way to control the exploitation of the working class, producing a collection of writings published under the title of 'Women In Industry: From Seven Points of View (1908), edited by Gertrude Tuckwell and Constance Smith, to which both Mary Macarthur and Clementina Black contributed. Constance Smith praised the passage of the Bill on its second reading in the House of Commons, on February 21st, without division, and made a vigorous argument that the minimum wage was the only fair way forward for all concerned; answering the argument that:

" 'Weak and tottering industries will be destroyed'. Need we regret such destruction? Where sufficient capital for the safe and proper maintenance of an industry does not exist, and the business lives by the sweating of the men and women who work in it, the sooner it disappears the better. A man who finds himself unable to pay his employees a living wage, has no right to be an employer. We may pity his personal failure to achieve economic success; but elementary principles of right and wrong, no less than every plea of expediency, demand that he should relinquish an attempt to reach that success by exploitation of his fellow creatures."

On the other side of the fence were the employers; both the large manufacturers and the smaller factories, and middlemen. The industry comprised of some thirty large factories which were the main manufacturers of the largest gauge chain. They employed 1,500 men on the agreed rates, and were considered the fairer employers (Blackburn 1987). Then there were a group of much smaller manufacturers employing 200 or so, who were not particularly well treated or well paid. Then the domestic outworkers 2,000 mainly women who were controlled by 140 middlemen/women; whose unscrupulous practice and foul treatment had reduced most of these women to penury.

The 'foggers' exploitation had caused industrial problems which could no longer be ignored by the rest of the industry, who up to this point had allowed – many write encouraged – this mass exploitation for their own benefit. While the 'foggers' continually undercut one another, in order to make their profit, the poor women were stretched more and more to be able to produce enough chain to receive the same money that they had. This need to have to produce more for the same, had dramatic effects on quality. Customers began to return chain, or refused to buy more from the manufacturers, stating that the chains were useless; one can only assume that the links were fracturing and welds were breaking.

The Chain Manufacturers Association was comprised of the main manufacturers, who saw their profits becoming effected by the severe drop in quality leading to bad customer relations. They had very little philanthropic concern for the condition of the outworkers, whom they considered were in their dire state due to a 'moral problem' accentuated by their 'intemperance' (Blackburn 1987). The CMA divorced themselves from all social responsibility towards this section of the working population, preferring to live in their ignorant comfort in the neighbouring areas of Stourbridge. However, they did realise that checks and balances had to be enforced against the domestic section to control the excesses of the 'foggers' manipulation of them, in order to bring back some level of quality to production.

The CMA were not natural partners to the National Anti-Sweating League, but began to show active support towards the aims of the League for effective legislation to control sweating; the manufacturers perceived this intrusion by the socially-active middle classes as a means to an end for their problems. As far back as 1901, prior to actual formation of the League, there seems to have been some dialogue between the CMA and J. J. Mallon, who had begun to view their concerns over the need to be more inclusive towards the outworkers as a 'public spirited' act (Blackburn 1987).

It was in some small part that the CMA's activities promoted the cause of the scheduling chainmaking as one of the test cases to fall under the auspices of the new Trade Boards legislation, even encouraging a local MP Mr A. G. Hooper to speak in favour of the second reading (Blackburn 1987). In fact by 1909 the public face of the CMA was doing everything that it could to be openly vocal in its support for the proposed Act. The secretary of the CMA, Mr George Williams, was explicit in his support when he told the visiting Trade Boards officials, that his organisation was committed to the eradication of sweating in their trade (Blackburn 1987).

The actual fact was far from the truth, as would be proved through the forthcoming actions of the CMA, that they viewed the legislation as a tool to bring control into their industry. They realised that there were simply too many 'foggers' chasing a finite amount of work, which was decreasing weekly due to the strangling of the new recession. When this legislation was passed into law, and when their trade became scheduled, they would be able to impose rates which would make it impossible for many to survive, pushing the 'foggers' out of work and in many cases forcing them to leave the area. This would enable a rationalisation of the industry as a whole, as many would have to stop working. They did not perceive the female unions as a threat, because women had no rights or place in society, and besides, the history of unionism within the industry had meant that men had tended to protect their own interests through male trade unions, especially as work became less and rates were lowered.

The cohesive fight which had been waged by all those with interests in solving the problem of the sweated worker, had led to the Select Committee on Homework which was to hear evidence from many witnesses. It is easy in hindsight, to distil this episode to the few whom this story impacts on, but there were many contributors to that comprehensive body of evidence, and not just the most notable of this particular story. It is important to stress that this exploitation of the poor was a national problem that fed the gluttony of an avaricious, middle class society, and stretched into every corner of our isles. Through those months in 1907 the committee, led by its President Sir T. P. Whittaker heard from a large number of witnesses, on many aspects of the problem, which was estimated to affect 477,480 people.

There were factory inspectors who gave evidence on the appalling conditions of work in various locations around the country, such as the lace making in Nottingham, or an extensive report from one factory inspector from Birmingham, who covered; button carding, French polishing, electroplating, hook and eye carding. Gertrude Tuckwell gave evidence on the plight of the shirt makers, comparing their wages earned against goods sold. Mary Macarthur and Clementina Black gave evidence jointly on at least one occasion, claiming to represent twenty-five percent of organised working women (125,000), on the disparity of wages from town to town, for the same tasks.

The following year Mary Macarthur was giving comprehensive evidence from her blue book of individual cases. She highlighted such souls as Mrs A, the wife of a dock-labourer, who when he could work, earned 24s a week. They had five children and to supplement their income, she had worked a twelve hour day every day, for eighteen years, making blouses. This left no time for the woman to do her housework or look after the children, which her elderly mother would do, no doubt another mouth who had to be fed. Mrs A recorded that even though she was a quick worker she could only earn 9s to 11s a week and that she found that prices were getting lower all the time. She blamed the general state of employment for her plight as Mary relayed Mrs A's own words, "unemployment of men is one thing: so many men are out of work, and those firms have always got a long list behind them, and, therefore, they cut prices down because women go and beg for work."

Some of the evidence was treated with incredulity by the Committee about how these women actually survived, such as, Miss C who worked a nine hour day making baby linen, yet could only earn 7s and had to pay 6s and 6d for her rent. Or Mrs F who would average sixteen hours a day making shirts for 9 1/4d per dozen. She had six children to support and could only hope to earn 10s a week. When she was asked how she managed, she had replied, "we don't live, very often I used to go and sit at the machine all day without anything to eat.

By the 29th July of 1908 the evidence given to the Select Committee had been so compelling that three recommendations were given. Firstly, that there should be legislation in regards rates of pay for homework. Secondly, that in the first instance these rates suggested should be 'tentative and experimental'. Most importantly that there should be Trade Boards established in selected trades. This made the passage of the Bill that Sir Charles Dilke had fought so hard and long for through the House of Commons a foregone conclusion. In fact the National Anti-Sweating League had been so optimistic of the successful progress into law of this most necessary piece of legislation, that just a few weeks before it was passed in the following year, they had heralded this in The Morning Post 23rd July 1909:

> "The annual meeting of the National Anti-Sweating League was held yesterday at 10, Adelphi Terrace. Mr A. G. Gardiner presiding. In the third annual report, read by Mr Mallon, the hon. Secretary, the Executive Committee congratulated their fellow members on the completion of the first and perhaps most important stage of the road to the attainment of their object. The enactment of the Trade Boards Bill was no longer in doubt. In a few weeks, blessed by all Parliamentary voices, save a few that did not bless anything, the Bill would have become

an Act and in four trades at least Wages or Trade Boards would have begun their beneficent tasks. This is an outstanding outcome of less than three years' activity, and should encourage a much wider community of sympathisers to ally themselves with the League and assist it to the entire accomplishment of its task."

The first board to be assembled was the Chainmakers' Trade Board. It had been stipulated that each board should have representatives from the employers and employees alike. The employees' representatives were elected at a meeting held at Grainger's Lane School, in Cradley Heath on Monday 6th December, 1909. Mary Macarthur and Charles Homer were elected to represent the women chainmakers, and there were five others elected to represent male chainmakers; William Bate, Thomas Sitch, James Smith, William Cooper and Josiah Griffin; Sitch, Smith and Cooper were elected with larger majorities.

There were six employers' representatives; Mr W. Lashford-Griffin, Caleb Woodhouse, Noah Bloomer, G. H. Green, John Fellows and Joseph Woodhouse. Joseph Woodhouse was chosen to represent the middlemen/women. The Board was presided over by Mr W. B. Yates who was a barrister-at-law, with Mr Thomas Smith and Miss Mona Wilson. The inaugural meeting took place according to the Birmingham Gazette on the 7th January 1910.

From the outset it became clear to the employees' representatives, that the employers were not going to meet the challenge to set acceptable rates fairly. Meeting after meeting, broke up with no agreement, and obstructive behaviour on the part of the employers. As Barnsby (1998) writes the employers came with the arguments that any setting of rates that were too high would be detrimental to the very workers that the employees' representatives were there to protect:

"Employers could not afford higher wages; our expert trade would be lost: the trade would move abroad; women could not be employed thus creating unemployment; untold suffering would be caused by depriving women who were prepared to work for less than the Trade Board rate of employment."

The employers were absolutely agreed that any new rate set should not be too high as to damage their business interests (Blackburn 1987, Morgan 2001). Their real interests in securing the legislation for their trade had finally been exposed, and despite turning their arguments against the employees' representatives and couching their discourse in the damage that the unions were causing to the welfare of the workers, their only predetermination had been a purely selfish business interest.

Mary Macarthur and Thomas Sitch found the whole process to be extremely frustrating. They were cast in the role as giving advice to those employees' representatives who had very little experience of coming head-to-head with their own work-masters. The employees' representatives probably sat there with some fear and uncertainty of what the future would hold for them once the negotiations were complete; so much of the responsibility was weighted on Macarthur and Sitch. Ultimately, any agreement which could bring about a satisfactory end to negotiations would not be one fairly won, and as low as possible for the employers.

Two months of anguished and protracted meetings followed, where Mary Macarthur was certainly pushed to her physical and mental limits, as her biographer Mary Agnes Hamilton (1925) notes:

"Neither patience nor tolerance were natural virtues with her, and both were sorely tried, as meeting after meeting ended with no agreement and it looked as though the deadlock was insoluble. With her heart burning with a sense of the workers' sufferings, there were moments when the risk of failure was more than she could face."

In fact Hamilton (1925) records that after one particularly obstructive meeting failed yet again, Mary physically broke down in front of J. J. Mallon on a train to Nottingham that evening; having refused to take a lift from an employer to the station because of her undisguised anger and indignation.

When the final agreement was reached two months after the formation of the board, the rate was considered by the employees' representatives to be inadequate, but they had had to be capitulate to it, as the employers had forced the issue, Blackburn (1987):

"They agreed to accept it simply because the employers flatly refused to grant more and threatened to mechanize the industry."

This blatant arm twisting had forced the unions to accept a rate of 11s 3d per week for a fifty-four hour week, that equated to 2½d per hour (Blackburn 1987). On the face of things a significant increase of one hundred and fifty percent, but if we consider that the inflationary increases of a burgeoning recession were beginning to bite, it is a wonder if it actually did keep in line with the rise in the prevailing cost of living for that time. When analysing the Retail Price Index of the period leading to what we now call the 'Great Unrest', Barnsby (1998) is at pains to stress the enormous rise in the cost of living that this settlement was made in:

"One of the keys to this unprecedented period of militancy in Britain was the rise in the cost of living. Taking the Board of Trade Retail Price

Index as 100 in 1900, it rose slowly until 1906 and then jumped to 105; thereafter rapidly to 109 in 1910 and 115 in 1913."

Wages had already been appallingly low, but with general costs rising at such an acute rate, it is not hard to see that any agreement made – although better than previously – would soon have been outstripped by the rising prices.

However, any agreement that made things better for the workers, in such a hard-fought battle, was better than none at all; and the sense of history even at that point of time, that this was the first legal minimum wage, must have bolstered low spirits that anything could be possible from here on in.

In the TUC Archive, there is evidence of a draft of this agreement, with various edits and additions, it holds the complete tables – that I shall not give here – and contains the undertakings agreed:

"<u>Minimum Rates in the Hand Hammered Chain Trade</u>

In accordance with regulations made, under section 18 of the above Act, by the Board of Trade, and dated 27th April 1910, the Trade Board established under the Act for Hammered or Dollied or Tommied Chainmaking trade, HEREBY GIVE NOTICE, as required by section 4(2) of the above Act that they propose to fix [this is amended to have fixed] for the following minimum (or sweat) rates of wages.

Minimum time rate for hand-hammered chainmaking.

The minimum time-rate for making (for iron supplied by employers) Hand Hammered Chain up to and including 11/32" shall be 2½d per hour net and clear of all deductions where the employer provides, in addition to the iron, workshop tools and fuel on the premises where the work is carried on, but in all other cases the minimum time-rate shall be 3½d per hour net and clear of all deductions."

There follows after the tables three notes, the middle of which is crossed out, they read:

"The worker shall be deemed to produce 104lbs of chain from 112lbs or ordinary iron."

(The following note is struck through)

"The Trade Board will consider any objections, to the above rates which may be lodged with them three months from 16th May, 1910. Such objections should be made in writing and signed by the person making the same, who should add his full name and address, and should be sent to the Secretary of the Chain Trade Board, Office of Trade Boards, Caxton House, Westminster, London, S. W.

W. B. YATES."

"It is provided by the above mentioned regulations that:-
Every occupier of a factory or workshop or any place used for giving out work to outworkers shall, on receipt of this notice, post up a significant number of these copies thereof in prominent positions in every factory, workshop or place used for giving out work in such a manner as to ensure in each case the notice shall be brought to the knowledge of all workers employed by him who are affected there by.
    PENALTY for non-compliance, a fine not exceeding 40s."

One can only imagine the outrage that some employers must have felt when having these conditions enforced on them; the larger employers might be able to carry the burden of the rate increases, but the smaller factories may have found this the greatest of impositions. The 'foggers' would be behind the employers all the way, for as long as their discontent was evident, the 'foggers' were in some way protected from the enforcement of anything.

Sitch and Macarthur were naturally relieved that the process had been finalised but still angered by what had been a 'conceded agreement' in the end. It is recorded in the Manchester Dispatch (16.3.1910) and The Daily News (23.3.1910) as a 150% increase for the women, and most reports remained favourable for the rest of the month.

However, as Blackburn (1987) points out the CMA were not best pleased with what they considered to be a high settlement and decided to counteract by exploiting a 'loophole' in that agreement that they had identified in the legislation. The 'loophole' concerned Clause 5 which allowed for contracting out on the old rate for a further six months after the cooling off period of three months had elapsed. The agreement had been formalised on 17th May, 1910, and allowed three months before it would come into force, making the enforcement period mid-August.

The vast majority of working people in that area of the Black Country suffered from a high degree of illiteracy. It is certainly doubtful that many could read let alone understand the many notices of the new rates, which had been copiously pinned up on factory doors, and they probably relied on those (who were probably the 'foggers') with greater levels of understanding to reveal the contents. This illiteracy the employers used to their advantage. Waivers were drafted, which upon the outworker appending their mark, committed those outworkers to work for the old rates, from that August until the coming February. Those that refused to sign, were told that unless they did so there would be no work for them.

This blackmail and coercion would enable the employers to build up stock at the old rate in their yards for six months, as Blackburn (1987) writes:

"Their intention was to utilize their stocks, when the new rates became legally operative to make the majority of women unemployed and the Act unworkable."

As Hutchins (1915) observed from the position of the woman worker in Cradley Heath faced with this adverse pressure, whether she was in the union or not:

"Thus the workers were faced with probability of a period of unemployment and starvation, in addition to which a number of employers issued agreements which they asked the women to sign, contracting out of the minimum wage for a further period of six months."

Whether the women were forced through blackmail, or compelled through the prospects of being out of work and having families to feed, the deed was done. The employers knew that with the recession biting ever deeper, that there would be much less demand for their goods in the coming years and any stockpile that could be accumulated now would see them through until the market picked up again. Meanwhile, everything that they had desired from the legislation had come to pass, they would have the workers, working under exactly the same rates as before, for as long as they needed them, and then they would simply stop buying the chain from the middlemen. That would finish off much of the domestic industry and cull the large amount of outworkers and their handlers. Blackburn (1987) concludes the employers' motivations:

"The employers were confident that their plan would be a huge success for, unlike many other trades, the stock did not deteriorate, was easily warehoused, and did not like millinery for example, become unfashionable."

The strategy to force unemployment and to whittle all those who would not stay, would mean generally the older, more experienced (more dependent) remaining, and if and when, the industry recovered, the quality would improve dramatically; the employers considered that they had won in their eyes; but they did not allow for one woman, whose drive and determination would not let this go.

Some have analysed that which happened next was as much about the need for self-publicity that placed Mary Macarthur centrally, however, one telling comment that she had written several years earlier leads me to believe that Mary Macarthur would never have taken on a fight willingly if it could have been avoided, in fact, she has been quoted as saying that she would not undertake any strike she could not win:

> "It is quite a mistaken idea that strikes are caused by trade unions. As a matter of fact, strikes amongst unorganised workers are much more frequent, although the world do not so readily hear of them. A trade union really tends to prevent strikes by removing the grievances which cause them."

(Mary Macarthur, 1908)

A fair comment indeed, and one that employers might well have been better to have taken on board in the first place. The settling of the first minimum wage had set a historical precedent, but one that was highly volatile and liable to be destroyed by these malicious actions. If the minimum wage went through and became established, it would be a domino effect for every other sweated trade to follow. There were too many interested parties and keen observers to allow this course to founder because of the actions of a few employers bent on a selfish act. And Mary Macarthur with the whole vanguard of the women's trade union movement behind her, was on a crusade for the right of every working woman in the country; it had become a personal fight for her, having already suffered the humiliations that she had with these same men.

Chapter 9

THE 'LOCK OUT'

"In attempting to organise women there is, as in everything else, a psychological moment – a tide which must be taken at the flood. It is significant that many successful organisations recently formed have been the results of some sudden encroachment on the rights of workers."

(Mary Macarthur, 1908)

The most important outcome of this strike, is not that it was won, it is that it was not lost; there was simply too much to lose. The whole outcome of industrial relations history would have been altered dramatically had this strike not achieved all that it set out to do. It was not just a large group of women striking for the right to a legally set and agreed rate for their work, it was not just a trade where sweating had proliferated and been brought sharply to the public's attention; it was the first step on the ladder for the rights to universal suffrage for every exploited worker, whether man or woman.

What happened at Cradley Heath affected the lives of thousands of other workers at that time and led to a growing self-awareness among the traditional underclass, leading to what we now know as the 'Great Unrest'. The period when those that had suffered in the grip of the oppression of poverty and grossly manipulative employers, began to rise up to seek restitution and recognition. In fact it can be argued, that the ramifications of the Cradley dispute go much further and stretch out historically. Even today, like the ripples in a pond from a stone, the effects of Cradley Heath have impacted on our modern society, and without that moment in history the movement of change may well have been delayed quite considerably.

The Chainmaking Trade Board had met three months earlier and agreed the increased rate, which although it could be acclaimed as a substantial increase, was not considered by the unions to be the level that their members were entitled to. The employers on the other hand, who were reluctant to pay any increase whatsoever, knew that they had to make some sort of concessionary rise, however, they could already see when the agreement was being drawn up, a section of the agreement which they could use to their advantage to enable them not to have to pay the increase in the short term and be able to stockpile for a longer period; if all went their way they could cull the industry with one stroke.

According to many authors, the main employers 'colluded' with the 'foggers' to have them take round 'waivers' or agreements to contract out of the new rate for six months to all the domestic outworkers. If a woman refused to sign she was told that there were many who had, and she would lose out because she would not be given work; most women had no idea what they were signing and appended their marks totally innocently, probably assuming that they were signing for the increase.

The stockpile of chain at the old rate began to appear in the employers' yards as the chainmaking continued throughout that three month period, but few knew that even when the new rate came into force that it would be ignored and the old conditions would apply. The employers were content, for they had achieved what they wanted; the chain was still being produced cheaply, and they were able to stockpile it to ride out the new recession. Meanwhile, when they closed their gates after six months to all chain, they knew that would finish the industry. The 'foggers' would move towns to find some other sweated trade to exploit, and the many chainmakers unemployed would eventually turn their hands to something else or leave; after a time when the market picked up, the employers would have very few left to make chain. The employers would be able to pay them what they wanted – because the act would have become unworkable – they would be the older more dependent workers, with greater experience, and more willing to work for less; and because of their greater experience there would be a dramatic improvement in the quality of chain.

The union had either been unaware of the foul practice of forced waivers, or had chosen to ignore it until they were in a position to act. On the 23rd August the union drafted their agreement that all of their members must be paid the agreed rate. The employers were incandescent but had the rights of the signed agreements to contract out on their side; and proceeded to lock-out the women. The process of lock-out meant that the women were locked out from the yards to collect the iron to make the chain; and for those women who rented workshops from the middlemen they were locked-out of those, or if they rented tools and a block, they were removed. Effectively all of their access of earning a living was denied to them.

According to Barnsby (1998) the general lock-out was declared by the employers on the 27th August, of all workers, because many of the women had refused to sign the agreements. Although the Daily Express (22.8.1910) records that one thousand women engaged in Cradley Heath were 'due to be locked-out' and the Dundee Courier (23.8.1910) confirms that the minimum wage order was effective from August 17th. Blackburn (1987) writes that:

"The union retaliated by calling on strike those women who were working for less than the new rate. By the evening of Thursday, 1 September, the number of women on strike totalled nearly eight hundred, barely half of whom belong to the union."

This was a remarkable call-to-arms by the union; Sitch, Varley and Macarthur at the head, however, non-union members were going to pose a problem from the outset. A union's strike fund (and access to that fund) was based on a principle of due-paying members subscribing through insurance. Many of the women in the Cradley Heath agitation had not joined the union, simply because they could not afford to pay their dues in the first place. It did mean that for those that were, there was access to strike pay from the outset; and those women would be able to stay out as long as necessary, but still bring much-needed income into their homes. For the non-union members, there was effectively no money, an issue that had not escaped Mary Macarthur and one that she acted on almost immediately from day one of the lock-out.

During that first week they marshalled the women, firstly a procession was held in the High Street, where a rally call was given and the women sang 'Onward Christian Soldiers' as they marched. This culminated with the opening of the strike offices; where Charles Sitch and Charles Homer would officiate for the duration of the strike. Mary Macarthur was there and ready to rouse the women to fight, a meeting was called at Grainger's Lane School on the 23rd August; Thomas Sitch presided, supported by Mary Macarthur; J. J. Mallon was in attendance representing the National Anti-Sweating League, Julia Varley represented the Birmingham branch of the NFWW, and Charles Sitch was the representative of the local branch of the NFWW.

Sitch poured praise on the women who had not signed the agreement for standing up to the employers. Macarthur is quoted in the Midland Evening News (Wolverhampton – 23.8.1910) as saying that Cradley Heath was a 'black spot' and the union was 'compelled to do all they could to remove that stain'. According to The Daily News of the same date 'Miss Macarthur was loudly cheered when she counselled resistance, and a gaunt, tall woman elicited loud approval when raising her head aloft; she undertook "to drop dead rather than sign".'

This was the start of the constant barrage of publicised action that the union would take over the coming weeks. Mary Macarthur knew that the media would be the best way of bringing the nation's sympathy behind this small dispute in the Black Country, and she adopted this strategy of high press exposure from the very outset, in order to bring significant pressure on the employers that they had least expected. They hardly had time to draw breath before two days later the Midland Evening News (Wolverhampton – 25.8.1910) was reporting the procession of 800 women that had taken place in the Loomey Town that day which had been addressed by Mary Macarthur and Julia Varley. In fact the Express and Star (Wolverhampton – 25.8.1910) was reporting that 'an audience of 3,000 assembled', and that the crowds had been informed that strike pay was to be issued the following Saturday. The Daily News of the same date, reported that the assembled women and girl chainmakers chanted 'We never, never, never will give in; no we wont.' Julia Varley was quoted praising the NFWW, for she could only find 50 women who had actually signed the agreement.

Meanwhile, the employer's counter-volleys were almost lost in the loud publicity from the union. George Williams made an attempt to dispute the foundations of the strike initially, but his complaint was barely audible above the din of euphoria being generated from the women chainmakers nationally. His main argument for being unable to control what was being offered to the women was that many of the 'outsiders' (middlemen) could not be forced to pay the new rates until that six month period had elapsed; they were not members of the CMA, thus out of his control. Of course, the CMA had no intention of enforcing even then, their strategy would be turn any work away and simply not buy it.

The pressure from the union to raise the dispute in the public's consciousness was relentless, according to Barnsby (1998), 'further mass meetings were held'. There was one where Thomas Sitch had asked for a show of hands of all those that had not signed the agreement 'every hand went up'. At the same meeting Mary Macarthur had again called the women to action:

"Mary Macarthur then spoke and said that Cradley Heath was renowned around the world as a place of hard, dirty work for low wages. They wanted to alter this so that women had some chance of leading a happy life and not be treated as slaves."

The Union understood that there were two key factors that had to be addressed if they were to have any chance of winning this dispute, especially if it became protracted and drawn out. Firstly, they had to maintain the morale of the strikers, through whatever means that they had at their disposal, secondly, they had to find funding, and quickly, for all those women who were not entitled to strike pay. Many were already facing having no food on their tables the following week unless this matter was addressed with some urgency.

The first problem was dealt with on a personal level, for instance, bringing Mary Stocks from the London NFWW to personalise the fight for the women, by teaching them a raft of songs especially written to well-known tunes; which they would learn by rote to sing at all of their rallies and marches (some of which I have included in the appendices). Songs, to the popular tunes of 'Daisy Daisy' and 'All the nice girls love a sailor' (Barnsby 1998). Secondly, they had to maintain as much positive publicity as possible.

On the 26th August, 1910, an appeal letter for funds began to appear in all the national newspapers, starting with The Times, a copy of the letter appeared in The Birmingham Mail that same day. It came directly from the NFWW and was written by Gertrude Tuckwell and signed by; Gertrude Tuckwell, David Shackleton (secretary NFWW) and Mary Macarthur. It appealed for donations to aid the non-union striking women, it received high profile coverage that day, appearing in; The Morning Post, The Daily News and The Westminster Gazette. It had results, within two days according to The Weekly Dispatch, the first substantial contribution had been received from a person of some standing; the Countess of Beauchamp sent a cheque for £100.

The local press began to add their social analysis of what was now becoming a nationally featured story, firmly placing the spotlight over that region of the country. Birmingham had received acclaim as the 'best governed city in the world' and perceived itself to be more socially equal than the neighbouring Black Country. The Birmingham Mail (29.8.1910) made strident commentary:

"That we should permit women to engage in such an arduous form of toil is not altogether a tribute to the chivalry of the nation. That they should continue to engage in it under conditions that have made the chain making industry the 'classic' sweated trade of the country is a disgrace not only to the employers who impose such harsh conditions upon their work people but to the nation which permits it."

The first week of the strike ended with strike pay being distributed to all the union members, it was a remarkable sum of 5s. most had never cleared that amount having worked a heavy week, after all their hefty deductions for; rent, tools, iron and fuel, they were flabbergasted to receive the sum without having to have lifted their hammers once during that time. However, the unions' optimism of a swift resolution was fading, as Barnsby (1998) notes:

"The following week hopes of a short struggle were waning. The union declared that it could not take unlimited responsibility, although it would do all that it was legitimately within its power to see that no one worked under price. But the employers could end the dispute immediately by only accepting chain with a certificate to say the minimum rate had been paid."

This received very little reaction from the employers. The union persisted they knew their highest priority was to address the plight of the non-organised women, who were effectively facing starvation whilst the others were receiving strike pay. In all probability this is where them employers were hoping that the strike would fail, as the unions struggled to find funds for so many non-union members. Mary Macarthur took the opportunity of the generous donations of the Countess of Beauchamp and others, to put Cradley Heath at the centre of news stories yet again. According to Barnsby (1998) 'she made a flying visit' on the Monday, and being met at the station by an organised procession, she made her first press statement of that day, Barnsby quotes Macarthur:

> "Surely one of the most pathetic manifestations to our sense of liberty ever seen. For so long these women have gone on slaving for a pittance that some find it almost impossible to believe that they are actually being enabled to stand up for themselves."

The union made full advantage of the assembled press gathered and after having another procession through Loomey Town, Mary Macarthur was able to announce that because of the generous donations that had been made that 6s per week would be paid to all union members and 4s per week to all non-union members. It was a triumph of action that not only lifted any flagging spirits of those assembled, but brought the focus very firmly on their plight, as Macarthur qualified the situation saying, 'The eyes of the world are on Cradley Heath' (Barnsby 1998).

The employers resorted once again to the argument that they were not at liberty through the CMA to enforce the middlemen to honour the agreement. By this stage in the proceedings, the middlemen were beginning to feel the pressure of the bad publicity that was falling ever-increasingly on their shoulders. Their spokesman Joseph Woodhouse, who had sat on the original Chain Board, issued a categorical denial that they had been instrumental in this course of action and had not been aware of the possibility to be able to contract-out until they had been made aware of this by the larger employers; who in turn had provided the forms for them to do so (Barnsby 1998).

A flurry of press articles ensued firmly on the side of the strikers. The Birmingham Dispatch (30.8.1910) announced that the 'special lock-out fund' had already made £309. The Birmingham Mail of the same date made an astonishing announcement that:

"Mr Edward Cadbury has forwarded a letter of sympathising with the women in their struggle and promising a donation of £5 weekly towards the fund as long as the dispute continues."

Although the Cadburys did not actively support trade unions or strikes, they could support non-union members. By the 31st August, 1910, the union were announcing that they had £700 in their strike fund, but would need a fund of £1000 to pay their non-union women. The same day The Morning Post had publicised the unions' efforts to meet the needs of the non-union women with 4s. per week, and the Birmingham Mail gave figures that the strike currently had '330 unionists and 318 non-unionists.' There was a clear story developing for every person to read across the country, it portrayed a small union fighting valiantly for a group of hard-pressed women, whom the vile employers had tried to avoid paying a legally-agreed rate to. It was the employers who were avoiding their responsibilities to their workers, all they had to do was honour them.

Of course, the employers had no intention of meeting the unions on these terms, however, the national interest had rather caught them by surprise and in all probability angered them immensely, that they were being portrayed as slave masters nationally. They had viewed themselves as respectable businessmen carrying out an honest trade, that had been exploited by the many middlemen that operated in the industry, slicing off the profits for themselves. The CMA were struggling to be heard above the hubbub that was being generated by the union and decided to comply with the request by the Chain Board to meet with the union ten days after the strike had commenced, Friday 2nd September; the Chain Board would sit in the meeting in an arbitrating capacity.

The motivations of the CMA to become involved were not altogether as transparent as they might first appear; they were suddenly faced with a whole collection of consequences of their action that they had never considered, as Blackburn (1987) outlines:

"In the first instance they had not foreseen the enormous support which the women received from all classes of the public. Secondly, they had not reckoned with the resolve of the women themselves to fight for the new rates. Thirdly, the CMA was disturbed by the boycott being placed on their chains, and finally, they began to see the strike as an opportunity of removing the middlemen from the trade."

Indeed, the wealth of support was evident in the strike fund, which was accumulating daily, even in the form of street collections that were being made in Birmingham, as well as the generous donations being publically made by those of influence. Not only were the employers aware that they were in the public spotlight, but there were being scrutinised by many powerful people who were making judgements about them.

The employers had never been faced with such an organised campaign by a union, and one of such a national profile. All their previous experience of unions had been at a purely local level, disputes that were kept to their areas; generally settled to the advantage of the employers. The unions had made small inroads but never managed any comprehensive stand; and that was the male trade unions. The male employers had always dismissed the women as irrelevant, they had never been organised successfully and posed no particular threat of the status quo in the industry; in fact women were ten-a-penny and plenty more could be found to replace them. That was the way every part of the trade had always treated the women, just as an add-on, rather than a worker in her own right.

The CMA had never banked on the women being organised and remaining organised, as had been proved in other industries and to some extent in Cradley; if women were not paid adequately they could not afford to pay union dues and so would put that as their last priority; thus they became non-organisable. The extent to which the NFWW was prepared to go to, to assist and support these strikers had been astounding; and the strength of the individual women involved surprising. Most men in the society of the Black Country had probably never encountered a woman with as much presence and determination as Mary Macarthur; they had assumed their own rights to male authority as being ultimately victorious.

The bad publicity which was accumulating daily, was having an extremely detrimental effect on the actual sales of chain; many customers who had previously been loyal, wished to disassociate themselves with the tarnish of involvement with such a 'bad' industry. This was not necessarily because these individual customers had suddenly acquired a social conscience or even had not known the conditions previously; simply because mud has a nasty way of sticking, this one story in a paper might cause too much interest in another industry, and shine a light of inspection too closely there. Then there were the smaller simple customers, the shops and the ironmongers; solidarity amongst those who had little, probably helped the strike in some small way.

Following this, was the sudden dawning of realisation amongst the CMA that what they had worked for through their own strategy, to downsize the industry and increase the quality by the elimination of as many middlemen as possible, was actually achievable through the strike action. The adverse publicity which had been turned on the employers – which the CMA was doing its level best to refocus on the middlemen – could do the job for them. As long as this focus remained on those identified as unprincipled, exploiters of human life, the industry would be culled; many would have no work, or simply leave.

The meeting was arranged for the employers (via the CMA) and the union, arbitrated by the CTB, at the Cradley Heath Council Offices. Whether it was a deliberate strategy of the employers to protract the strike – to break it, or force the 'foggers' out – we will never know. The employers came with an unworkable solution that they knew the union could not meet; they would 'do all in their power' to ensure that the new rate was paid as long as the unions would subsidise all those women by 4s per week, who would not work under the rate for the six months period of contracting-out (Barnsby 1998).

This was financial ruination for the union at that point and could not be agreed to; besides which the employers were not making guarantees that the rate would be definitely paid (after all they had been insisting that they could not enforce an outsider – middleman to pay). They were merely undertaking 'to do all that they could' to ensure the rate was honoured. The meeting broke up without resolution and was adjourned until 10th September, the strike was set to continue.

That same day the union decided to mount what would be a 'first' for publicity of any dispute, and what would become a regular feature of all future newsworthy events. The NFWW had made contact with Pathe Cinematographers in London to come and record the event for publication in their news theatres. The Birmingham Mail that day confirmed the event thus:

> "A procession was held this afternoon, and arrangements were made for cinematographer films to be taken by a London firm, in order that the pictures of the strike could be produced at London picture palaces. It is also hoped to make a collection at theatres and music halls."

One can only wonder at the amazement that the locals of Cradley Heath must have felt to have such an event take place in their tiny town, which up till then had seen very little excitement; and we can only speculate on the amusement and oddity of the photographers from the local and national press, photographing the spectacle of the cinematographers, recording the strike. By that time in the dispute, Barnsby (1998) records that the strike had generated considerable interest in media quarters:

> "The civic pride of Cradley Heath was being ruffled by 'hordes' of reporters descending on the town and seeking out its worst aspects."

That evening, as had now become a feature of most evenings, the women were once again assembled to hear speeches from their visitors. This time Julia Varley gave a rousing address, and followed by George Shann (the co-author of Edward Cadbury's social investigations), who stood in for Edward and rallied the women to the cause of the sweated across the country.

Julia Varley had decided it was time to confront the rich neighbour and her branch area, with the shame of what they had for so long ignored. She organised a small team of women to come with her to Birmingham to take collections in the streets, especially around the Bournville area of the city; where George Cadbury had his, now famous, village. She chose her women with great thought for the maximum impact upon publicity. Three of them were of great age; Patience Round 79 years having worked sixty-nine in the forge, Olive Grasser 71, and Esther Totney who was not sure of her own age, she guessed it to be between 63 and 65.

The women were taken from the drab harsh conditions of Cradley Heath and led to the garden suburbs of Birmingham; they were as much amazed about what they witnessed that day, as any of the onlookers and well-wishers were of them. Among the many donations – totalling £13 – they received a red rose, and a green apple, which the women had probably never seen before. Julia met with Birmingham Trades Council on the 5th September as a member of the same, she used it as a platform to vent her spleen as regard the duty that Birmingham should take to support the strikers. The Daily News (5.9.1910) quotes the following:

'Miss Varley added a few pointed sentences, "The old book says," she remarked, "that the eyes of the fools are on the ends of the earth. That is where the eyes of the Birmingham people are when they could be nearer home. Birmingham has neglected the cry of the women of Cradley Heath too long. It is the nearest big industrial centre, and yet I have had to bring 15 chainworkers here – the youngest was 60 and the eldest 79 – to convince Birmingham people that their help is needed".'

This was a direct challenge given not just by Julia Varley, and not just by the NFWW, but by all those connected with the struggle in whatever capacity – whether the NASL, or the political contacts, or the social philanthropists – to make Birmingham accountable in the face of adverse publicity for their inactions. It is particularly interesting at this stage in the strike to speculate on the connection with the Cadbury family.

Obviously as Quakers they could not be seen to be supporting any union activity, and the donation that had been given at this stage by Edward Cadbury had been donated in support of the non-union members. George

Shann had come to speak in Edward Cadbury's place, as he had a prior engagement; he was reportedly careful in how he framed his support for the strike – more as support against sweating than for strike action. Julia Varley having sat on the Birmingham Trades Council a while, and being based in Birmingham, had ample contact with both these individuals, they probably shared many mutually-held beliefs.

She chose to take the women to Bournville, for what reason? She could have chosen any other part of the city, there were many more central areas of Birmingham to expose these women to publicity and affluence. Was she encouraged by the Cadbury family to visit there for a mutually beneficial share in publicity? Did she do this action to provoke George Cadbury into some active involvement? After all he had stayed very quiet to this point in time. He had undoubtedly supported the National Anti-Sweating League and continued to act as its President, and his newspaper – The Daily News – was being exploitatively used by Mary Macarthur to cover the strike. One would have drawn the natural conclusion that he should have, by that time, become overtly involved, yet he appeared to have nothing to do with it at this stage.

Maybe in one of the many discussions and meetings that had taken place between Edward Cadbury, George Shann and Julia Varley in their various trade and civic capacities, it may have been suggested that it might be necessary to apply a little pressure on Mr Cadbury senior to tie his colours to the mast, and come out and overtly grant strike support? I speculate that up until this stage in the strike, no influential Birmingham family had shown any substantial support for the strike, I am not saying that the Cadburys had not, maybe they were very quietly trying to encourage others to take a more active role, rather than placing all of the social responsibility on their shoulders, as had so often been the case.

It is possible that Edward needed his father to be more open to try and attract all of those other great entrepreneurial families who had a tight grip on the Birmingham business-sector to be more forthcoming. Julia was in Bournville for a reason, I do not believe it was purely a coincidental act. However, as we shall determine in the next chapter, although the strike endured for some weeks, there is no doubt that this connection to the Cadburys and the publicity visit to Bournville, focussed the attentions of many and galvanised the actions of a few.

Chapter 10

UNITED WE STAND TOGETHER

The Cradley Song – "Raise Ye Women"
(Tune – Men of Harlech)
Raise, ye women, long enduring,
Beat no irons, blow no bellows,
Till you win the fight, ensuring,
Pay that is your due.

Chorus

Through years uncomplaining
Hope and strength were waning –
    Your industry
    A beggar's fee
A meagre fare was gaining
Now a Trade Board is created
See your pain and death abated
And the sweater's wiles checkmated
Parliament's decree!
      (The Cradley Song – full version in the Appendix IV)

Whether Edward had planned to be at the Empire Theatre in Cradley Heath that night, and Julia had gone to Bournville to capitalise on that opportunity for publicity, we shall never know. However, that evening of the ladies day out collecting on the streets of Birmingham, Edward Cadbury was the main speaker at the theatre in Cradley Heath, the crowds now surging to come to rallies; which had been vastly swelled by journalists and many other curious individuals from other places, could no longer be contained in the very modestly sized Grainger's Lane School, it was thought the theatre a far more fitting location for what was now an international story.

Julia Varley presided over the meeting and was ably supported by both Thomas and Charles Sitch among others. Charles reported to the assembled crowds that there had been no change to the employers' position, according to the Birmingham Gazette (6.9.1910). When Edward Cadbury rose to speak all assembled listened intently to what he had to say, the Birmingham Gazette records thus:

"Mr Edward Cadbury, who was heartily received, said he had come to show his sympathy. He had a message from his father, Mr George Cadbury, who wished him to say how he sympathised with them, and who had promised a contribution of £10 per week. (Loud applause.) His father had long been interested in the question of sweating, and was largely responsible for the Anti-Sweating Exhibition, which was the means of bringing the evil prominently before the country. He (the speaker) felt that that strike was different from an ordinary strike, as he considered it to be an antiquated way of settling a dispute. He characterised that strike as an important one, as they were in the forefront for the movement of carrying out a minimum wage fixed by the State. They had a good trade to bring the Act into force, and if it could not be done by the chain trade it could not be with any other. The women were asking for 2½d an hour, or 11s a week, and that was a modest wage for the heavy work. He hoped that it would remain at that figure. He had the management of 3,000 women, and in their business they considered that no women over 20 working 44 hours a week should receive less than 16s a week. (Applause.)"

The next day many papers carried the story of the Cadburys' generous support, as well as other articles which were copiously supplied by Mary Macarthur, who had kept up a steady stream of stories about her observations of the lives of the women in Cradley Heath. In articles such as 'Slaves to Forge', Mary drew an evocative picture for the reader of the life of sheer drudgery that each woman faced from the minute she turned into an adolescent to the point of her death. One of the main themes that Macarthur was extremely good at emphasising was the loss of youth and freedom that the women experienced. I have quoted previously, her observation of the 'saddest sight' being for her seeing young girls entering chainmaking before they had any chance to live. The girls themselves felt little sadness if any, for it was an expectation that they would become chainmakers, and they had to achieve a certain amount in a week to be a good chainmaker, and they knew that. They had enormous sense of pride and achievement. But Macarthur, the external viewer, reacted as all of her middle class peers would, with disbelief that a youth was somehow cut short, never to be regained and the beauty of that youth gone too. Always, as if to bring the stark comparison to the reader's attention immediately, she would compare the life of the young with the fatigue of the old:

"I do not know which is the more pitiable, the tragedy of the young or the tragedy of the old. In the present 'lock-out' there are fifteen women over sixty, and scores over fifty years of age. The oldest is seventy-nine. She has worked at chain-making since she was ten, she tells you in her quavering voice. Her children and her children's children are all slaves to the forge. The other day came the great adventure of her life. She went with others to Bournville to collect money for the 'Lock-Out' Fund from her more fortunate sister workers at Cadbury's Garden Factory. It was the longest journey that she had ever made in her long life. What a wonderful day it was! She came back with a full collecting-box, and, greater treasures still, a red rose and a green apple. She told us in a hysteria of pathetic delight of all the marvels she had seen. Later on I talked to a score of old women gathered at the corner of the street. Not one of them had ever seen the sea."

As with so many of the reports that were generated to keep up the pressure on the general public, the union realised how the facts and figures of chainmaking were some of the most thought-provoking and used these to their ample advantage, 'Slaves to the Forge':

"Take one chain chosen at random – No. 6 coil. The manufacturers themselves estimate that to earn 10s. a week on this chain a worker must weld over 5,000 links. Each link requires at least ten blows from the hammer. A week's work means, then, more than 50,000 blows. And the bellows must be blown and the forge attended to, the iron rods lifted. The iron must be carried from the warehouse to the workshop and the finished chain carried back again. And for this the women ask 10s. To many of them that spells riches. One woman reckoned the other day that at the old prices she had to strike a thousand blows to earn three-halfpence."

These were the themes that would be returned to, again and again, by the union publicity machine which was rolling under the watchful eye of Mary Macarthur. She was determined that the British public would have the pitiful story ever present in the collective psyche and not for one second would they be allowed to forget; there was not going to be a dry eye in the house by the time she had finished. On the 6th September, alongside the many reports of the triumph of Edward Cadbury's visit to the Empire, there were still the stories twisting at societies heart strings, such as this in the Yorkshire Evening News:

" "Tiny hands at Cradley Heath," says Miss Macarthur "take hold of iron as happier ones take hold of flowers." Old men and women declare that they cannot remember the time when they could not "shut a link"."

By far one of the biggest publicity coups that the union managed to stage throughout the duration of the dispute was one organised by Julia Varley; who seemed to have an eye for identifying from where the most newsworthy items could come. The Trades Union Congress that year was to be held in Sheffield, on Tuesday 13th September, the WTUL had a number of meetings planned to take place at Congress, Julia saw this as a brilliant opportunity to impact on the male trade unions at their very heart. By what is recorded it seems that she took her hand-picked three ladies (possibly Patience, Olive and Esther, although one is reported as younger). What an adventure it must have been for these three souls making the train journey to Sheffield; it must have been their farthest distance yet travelled. Arriving at the conference and knowing what they had to do, they must have been incredibly nervous. Probably, Julia would have explained that it would be like the Empire Theatre only bigger, and that they were not to be fearful, all the men there were very much behind them.

It was a symbolic message that they brought with them that day, before the national delegates of the Trade Union Congress. By all reports the congress was proceeding through the slow mundane business of that particular day:

"The talk about the internal economy of trade union organisation was dramatically interrupted by the chairman, who introduced three women from Cradley Heath – two elderly women and one younger. They were a deputation from the chainmakers, and brought chains with them on the platform. Raising her burden of chains and outstretching them, the younger women called out, 'We plead with you to help us get twopence-halfpenny an hour for making these. We mean to fight for it. We shall succeed if you help us.' 'We will,' shouted the Congress heartily. The chairman who described the chainmakers as 'poor white slaves,' proposed a resolution of sympathy with them, and promising monetary help. This was carried forthwith. A suggestion that the women should make a collection there and then was vetoed by the chairman, on the ground that it would be undignified, but a collection was taken before the congress adjourned for the day."

Two other special interest stories that found resonance with many well-wishers was one written by the 'special correspondent' for the Daily Express Mary Mortimer Maxwell (6.9.1910) and another item a day later (paper unknown) entitled 'Women of the Forge: a veteran striker'. Both stories described in detail the lives of the hard-pressed women; it seems that Patience Round had become a celebrity in her own rights as she was interviewed extensively for both stories. In the story by Maxwell, she describes the poor smiling children greeting her asking her for a 'nod', this she discovers is a cheap pastime of many who simply collect nods for wishes. When they have collected 'so many nods' they would record them on their scraps of paper, which were then secretly burnt in the ashes of their mothers' forges. The story gave a description of their mothers, whose hands were knotted and gnarled, yet one hand faired slightly better than the other as Maxwell discovers:

"The left hand wields the tongs. The right hand, which is used for swinging a hammer not particularly heavy, is very much smoother and better formed than the left."

The code by which they lived meant that a woman could not do the man's job of working the 'dollie', which enabled him to produce better work and to support his family. A woman could not cross that line and work with a 'dollie' because 'She'd be taking the bread out of other men's mouths'. These women placed themselves at the bottom of the wage earning society because that was the code by which they had lived. Patience Round who she describes as looking more like a retired dressmaker than a chainmaker of sixty-nine years; dressed in Sunday best. In the other story Patience makes a wistful account of her earlier years, her ceaseless work since she was a young girl; the yards of chain that she calculated that have now become thousands of miles. Her thoughts of old age which have become a further tie to the forge as she supports her ailing husband. The pathos of the way in which the very thing that she has been tied to all these years has now become a strange sort of comfort in her later years; the warmth and the mesmerism of the fires of the forge.

In that same article, the reporter records the unions lack of hope from any possible outcome with the CMA at the conference due to take place on the 10th September:

"The local secretary of the National Federation of Women Workers (Mr C. H. Sitch) stated yesterday that the outcome of the conference would not be a prompt settlement unless the employers offered other terms. The women's union, in order to meet the guarantees required by the Manufacturers' Association were in need of a fund amounting to at least £1,000 to begin with. It was estimated that £60 per week would be required to pay the non-unionists concerned in the dispute, and the number was increasing daily. The amount would also be advanced."

So it was not with a great sense of optimism that the union sat down for a second time with the CMA. In fact, it was a very intransigent CMA who met them, as Barnsby (1998) notes, George Williams was querulous, and mischievously enquired why so much was being collected for the strikers fund when it would end in a matter of weeks; the manufacturers had decided that work and employment would operate amongst themselves in future, making all the middlemen and outworkers effectively redundant.

As with all disputes that run into weeks, and then months, once the first wave of publicity has passed through and the end seems not to be in sight, it settles into a pattern, as it did with Cradley Heath. It was now the fourth week of the dispute, the union knew that it was as important to keep the strikers as committed to the fight as it was to keep the public interested and many friends were called upon to lend a hand with coming to Cradley to rally support; even the clergy were taking a keen interest following the lead made by the Cadbury family. The Bishop of Worcester was enthusiastic to show his support and had delegated the task of speaking on his behalf to his Dean (Dr Moore Ede). The chairman for that rally was chosen, quite understandably, from the serving local clergy – Rev. R. E. Walker (Vicar of Cradley Heath).

He used his platform to make some timely criticism of various aspects of the news reporting which had been describing his parish as 'near to hell'. He jumped to defend the town against what he considered to be gross-exaggerations of the truth. However, he did counter this by pointing to the facts that the need to free the women workers from enslavement was something that had his full support. He was also able to relay some very important news, although the meeting between the CMA and the union had brought no resolution, he was able to report that the manufacturers' were now in agreement to meet to minimum rate.

This as we know with hindsight and understanding, was the CMA talking for its members, which they had already qualified on several occasions was not a representation of the middlemen; whom the CMA regarded as a separate entity and a separate voice within the dispute. Consequently, after some explanation of the situation to those assembled, Rev Walker, roused the women to fight on and stand firm.

The Dean of Worcester delivered a similar message from the Bishop; who apologised for not being able to attend in person, but had enclosed a cheque within his letter for £5 towards the fund. The Bishop's letter was one of full support towards the women in their endeavours, not just to strike for the wage, but their generosity of spirit to stand beside their non-union friends. He was pleased to hear that the CMA had agreed on the minimum rate, but he used the opportunity to condemn those unwilling to pay. By now there was growing pressure on the middlemen to settle, they were being portrayed as the villains, rightly or wrongly, not just by the press, but now by the house of God. This would bring a new wave of public support very firmly to the strikers' cause.

Dr Moore Ede did make a social comment which drew a much broader net across the whole dispute, that of Empire. Birmingham had of course looked to their 'father' in Joseph Chamberlain, the once great Radical Liberal turned Imperialist, as his policies had been driven more to protectionism of the Empire, so the Caucus had turned too, it followed that there had been much imperialism to be found within the discourse of the local press. The Daily News (Midland Edition) 13.9.10:

> "Dr Moore Ede remarked that nowadays it was the fashion to talk about the British Empire, on which the sun never set. It was a great Empire, and they ought to be proud of it; but no true patriot could be proud of Cradley Heath and the conditions of the women's labour in that community of chainmakers."

This remark is even more interesting if one considers the sheer coincidence of what had occurred two days previously, when a letter had been received from Arthur Chamberlain, apologising that he could not offer any other help due to ill-health, but happily enclosed a cheque for fifty guineas.

While these few days had passed by, the CMA had begun to realise that they were placing themselves in an increasingly isolated position and as much as it galled them, they knew that they had to be showing some movement towards conciliation. A 'white list' had been drawn up of all those who had conceded to paying the minimum rate, reports had been varying over the days that 60% of the employers had agreed. The reports commented that all the main employers had agreed, even that these employers were willing to 'throw over' the middlemen in order to settle; that meant that 30 – 40 of the employers were of the same mind. However, they had not reached that position at the previous meeting and had been openly critical. Williams having been reported as saying that the money that union was collecting could not be used to support paying non-union workers; an accusation Mary Macarthur took issue with, and Williams then took actions to make an immediate retraction of his statement in a letter published on the 13.9.1910.

In his vitriolic defence of what had been written about him – quoting him saying that too much money was being raised – he made a number of swipes at Mary Macarthur; the implication being that the union was going to use the money for other activities elsewhere. It is obvious from the tone of this letter that relations between the two were neither constructive or cordial by this stage. Once again Williams does his best to portray the CMA as working on behalf of his members, who in turn are seeking to improve the situation of the domestic workers, he writes:

> "By the action of the members of the Employers' Association signing the white list and the influence that I know it will have and has already had on other manufacturers, and the number of signatures that I know I have obtained and promised to the white list, at least 60 percent. of the women affected must now be employed at the minimum rates, and in spite of stocks of chain, there certainly must be a very considerable number of women employed long before the expiration of the six months. Is there anything then very extraordinary or discreditable in my statement that if £1,000 is required to keep the whole of the non-union workers during the six months, £1,500 is sufficient in the present circumstances?
>
> However, if Miss Macarthur really thinks that a considerable amount more is required from the public for the non-unionists for the purposes of the present dispute. I do not in anyway wish to put any difficulties in her way, but was only making an obvious comment on her own previous figures."

The union was quick to come back in its own defence, by exposing this suggestion that the employers were about to agree as being a paper-thin claim. As Charles Sitch pointed out in the Wolverhampton Chronicle (14.9.1910), there were many more employers than just those allied to the CMA. The union, he claimed, had heard personally from a number of these other employers that they had no intention of paying the rate until the six months had elapsed. Even those who claimed to be signing up to the agreement were in many cases using 'tricks and dodges' to avoid honouring the payment of the new rate. The avoidance tactics that they were employing included; downgrading the quality of work being produced; insisting that there was no work available at the new rate; that they had heard from London that the new rate was not to be paid for six months; and even, paying it for a week and then reverting to the old rate – so that women had to come and re-sign the 'lock-out' list.

By week five, the middlemen had come out in their own defence of their position. As Barnsby (1998) notes (with an error naming him as Whitehouse), Joseph Woodhouse had rounded on the CMA saying as the majority of middlemen – accounting for ninety percent of the work – were willing to add their names to the list, that they would only do so if the CMA gave undertakings only to take work from them. Barnsby (1998) also notes that by this stage in the dispute '600 unionists were now working under proper rates with 140 unionists and 280 non-unionist still in dispute.'

This was the tenor of the strike for the coming weeks, claim and counter-claim. One side (normally the CMA) would claim that they were moving towards resolution, while the other (usually the union) would dispute the accuracy of any such statement. The only constant that had to be maintained was the morale of the workers on strike; a third of whom had now taken their opportunity for hop-picking to supplement their incomes. It was important more so now, as the strike dragged into its sixth week that momentum had to be kept going. It was the time that tensions were beginning to run high, as the end had still not been achieved, and the national publicity had gone; the only highlight having been the showing of the Pathe films in music-halls in London and the provinces which vast audiences had seen, and large collections had been made outside for the strike fund. Pathe estimated that the pictures would be shown in 500 to 600 provincial picture houses and London's principle music-halls; they expected an overall audience of up to 10,000,000 people. This was impressive publicity indeed, and tactic that would become common-place in many future high-profile events.

Now though, the strike had to some extent become old news, which presented new challenges to Mary Macarthur and her team; it was essential to keep spirits high in an attempt to retain the national spotlight in order to maintain the pressure on the employers. This included framing her own press interviews to show her pleasure for the moves that CMA were making towards settling, and how positive this all was for both the unions and the CMA if they could begin to identify those that were still refusing to pay. By now too, large local collections were being made on the streets and in the factories of Birmingham; Julia Varley and Edward Cadbury had drawn the populace of Birmingham into the need to support their sisters in the Black Country. The strike fund was standing at £1,500 with every expectation of it reaching in excess of £2,000.

In fact by the Sunday at the end of the sixth week, Mary Macarthur was able to announce to a packed audience of the Empire Theatre that the fund had reached £1,700; the union and the women must have felt an enormous sense of self-empowerment at now knowing that the struggle for financial support was no longer their first concern. Now the battle could truly focus on achieving a victory. At the same meeting according to Barnsby (1998) Arthur

Henderson MP and John Galsworthy made speeches to the assembled crowds. John Galsworthy was a renowned author; and some time later recorded his thoughts in his collection of works entitled 'The Inn of Tranquillity'; the story of Cradley Heath he entitled 'The Procession' (included in Appendix V). In this he evokes the atmosphere of the coming together of these simple souls to make their stand, in their Sunday best and shoulder to shoulder, marching, singing, and calling for their rights. He must have found considerable inspiration from what he witnessed on his visit to Cradley Heath that Sunday to speak, as the descriptive account shows.

At the same meeting, Mary Macarthur put the response of the CMA and the middlemen to the meeting and they voted to accept their proposals, with the plan to single-out any of those who had not signed and target them with 'guerrilla warfare' (Barnsby 1998). Later Mary Macarthur received some rough questioning at a meeting at Grainger's Lane School. People wanted to know if she agreed with some of the poor press that had been written about Cradley Heath, or whether she thought that the press had been too harsh?

She rounded on those present, pointing out that Cradley Heath was not a 'beauty spot', and she would be being hypocritical if she said that it was and defended the press reporting against their complaints of the towns-folk. She said that it was a place of greyness, with nothing for the children to do, and no enjoyment in the lives of the adults. According to Barnsby (1998) that was the moment that she conceived, and announced, the idea for the Workers' Institute to provide a centre for Education, Art and Enjoyment for the people of Cradley Heath. The residual funds from the lock-out would be used to help facilitate this.

However, the optimism of a swift end were dashed when relations between the CMA and the middlemen broke down, causing delays to any resolution, as the middlemen formed a breakaway organisation holding their meetings at Grainger's Lane, School. It is not difficult to analyse with hindsight the inevitability of the situation that had arisen. The CMA had effectively used the non-associated employers, the middlemen, as their excuse for, in the first place refusing to settle, and in the second place for their inability to settle the dispute. The CMA probably still held the desire to cull all the extraneous employers from the industry and de facto, putting the vast majority of domestic workers out of employment. So for as long as the middlemen continued to prevaricate this would make any resolution an unmanageable prospect. The middlemen were probably incensed by all of the bad publicity that had been placed at their door, which although they probably deserved in most cases, had been deflected by the CMA who were equally culpable for the sweating in the industry. As Blackburn (1987) notes:

"The CMA, which comprised many church and chapel-goers and local dignitaries, did not relish the title of 'sweater', and attempted to defend itself by stating that the reports of the women's position were grossly exaggerated. When impartial investigators concluded that this was not so, the CMA then declared that its hands were tied by unassociated members and middlemen."

The middlemen wanted to stop being controlled by, and at the behest of the CMA, so had decided to take action.

According to Barnsby (1998), the same venue was used for another meeting of the workers, who by this stage were becoming quite disheartened, even Mary Macarthur seems to have become resigned to not securing quite the victory that had first been hoped for. This is evident from the actions that were now considered at that workers meeting, including; picketing factory gates. She pulled short of agreeing to the workers demands of calling for a general strike, probably viewing this as a measure of last resort; this could drag out the dispute for months and by all probability break the Trade Boards Act. She knew that any measure such as national action was only something to be considered when all avenues locally had been explored and found wanting. She asked them to wait on the next meeting, which had been planned for October 19th, after which she promised 'drastic action' may be considered (Barnsby 1998).

The CMA were content, it seemed to them that responsibility for settling was no longer their problem; after all as George Williams pointed out in a letter his members had signed the white list, they could not compel 'non-associated members' to sign. The CMA placed the responsibility firmly in the hands of the union to find the settlement for their workers (Barnsby 1998).

According, to Mary Agnes Hamilton, in her biography of Mary Macarthur (1925), it was this breakaway organisation that in someway focussed the attentions of those non-associated employers to the scheming of the CMA. Those who were beginning to consider their own futures realised that the deadlock could effectively put them out of business, as Hamilton notes:

"...since once they got together they saw how easily the trade might be developed on lines that would crowd them altogether out."

Indeed, it is without doubt that Joseph Woodhouse began to use his own influence to persuade those that would that he could, that it was within their best interests to sign the white list, if they ever wanted to work again.

The following week the unions and the employers agreed on a resolution of working only with those who had signed the white list; if most had not signed on their own volition by then, it is certain that that must have been the final straw in compelling them to do so. Mary Agnes Hamilton (1925) evokes some of the tension that waited in the Grainger's Lane School room that night for Mary Macarthur and the others to come from the final conference to formulate the agreement with the employers, the air must have been electric. For when she did deliver her address from the platform, informing all who sat in front of her of the 'complete and decisive victory' in 'this most wonderful trade dispute' (Barnsby 1998), she was greeted with utter relief and jubilation, as Hamilton (1925) records:

> "At last she came. Wild applause greeted her: then tense silence again as the women listened, their eyes glued to the face of their deliverer: tears rising in many of those eyes and dropping, unheeded, down worn pale cheeks as they realized the fight was won."

The first minimum wage had been settled, 2½d per hour, a one hundred and fifty percent increase for the women who had slaved all of their lives, just to keep food on their tables, warmth in their homes and clothes on the backs of their children. It is easy now to say that this was not enough, that the effects of inflation would have wiped this increase away in no time, but for that moment, that one moment in the Grainger's Lane School room there had been a victory, one of which would impact throughout history, right through to the present day.

For those women, who had never had hope in their lives, they had been through an unbelievable journey of having very little (practically nothing) of not even possessing a personal identity. Within ten weeks they had become national celebrities, figures of interest that whole country poured out its sympathy and love for; the country showed them that it did care and that they did matter. That must have been for them all the most unimaginable feeling possible.

Chapter 11

THE AFTERMATH

What had occurred at Cradley Heath became a symbol of a raising up of the lower working classes from servitude; for the first time it gave hope to at least half a million people that they had a chance to rise above the oppression of their lives and seek a future. That is the key to all that happened from this point on. This victory lifted those who had previously never dared to dream of a different life; never believed that society cared enough to support them; in fact historically had been put-down. These poorest of the poor – the sweated souls – were now able to hope for more, and as an effect from that moment, became part of the society that they had always been disenfranchised from in so many ways.

At a local level the impact of the victory was much harder to gauge, although probably because of the psychological euphoria of having won; even if nothing had appeared in the wage packets of any consequence; the people were so buoyed-up that their lifted spirits changed the atmosphere of Cradley Heath. Barnsby (1998) writes that evidence of a new spirit of pride had returned to the hard-pressed little town, clothes were cleaner, children more presentable and wearing shoes; they were happy to show themselves off to the rest of the world now, they mattered. However, there was some evidence according to Barnsby (1998) of non-payment of the new rate, whether that was due to the unscrupulous middlemen, or the changes being lost in the 'myriad' of chain rates, is uncertain, this did not seem to dent the general lift in morale.

This may be as much to with the spotlight still remaining on this little town for some time to come. Mary Macarthur was true to her word and honoured her commitment to creating a centre for, education, training and leisure. The fund had remained open until the New Year and raised in excess of £3,000. After the costs of the strike had been met, the WTUL made a grant of £1,500 available for the building of the Institute in the town in Lower High Street,

In April, 1911, the WTUL sent a letter to all the benefactors who had kindly made donations to the fund, listing out their intentions for the remainder of the fund:

"The committee have taken into careful consideration the disposal of the surplus and have decided to apply two-thirds of the amount for the special benefit of women workers in Cradley Heath district by the building of a hall and institute, to be in trust for them, and the formation of a Contributory Scheme of Unemployed Benefit, especially for the older and less efficient workers who, in some cases, may suffer loss of work through the fixing of the minimum wage, and through the introduction of machinery in the future.

The Institute which it is proposed to erect in Cradley will, it is hoped, become a centre of social activity in the Black Country District. Educational meetings and lectures will be held. Here the women's union officials will have offices, and to them the workers will look for guidance in the thousand and one problems which arise inevitably from the operations of an experiment of such importance as the Trade Boards Act.

It is further proposed to divide the remaining third between the Women's Trade Union League, the National Federation of Women workers (to which organisation the women chain-makers now belong), and the Anti-Sweating League, in order that it may be devoted to the work of trade union organisation amongst women workers in other trades similarly situated to the chain-makers, for the assistance of any sweated women who may be involved in a similar dispute, and in the case of the Anti-Sweating League, for the development of its work in connection with the Trade Boards Act, and the securing of a legal minimum wage in additional industries to those already scheduled."

It must have been a difficult decision to, in effect, keep some of the money for what were essentially other activities: money which many others might well have viewed as the Cradley Heath Chainmakers' by rights. But it can be argued that without the comprehensive support that the chainmakers received from all three organisations listed, there would have been no strike fund and certainly no victory at Cradley. The Union and the League still had much to do in the achievement of their goals, and had probably drained much of their own funds pursuing the strike; this money would allow them to try and achieve the same outcome for a few more of those disadvantaged workers across the country, and as it turned out they were going to need it for exactly that, every last penny.

Two months later in June 1911, Mary Macarthur gave an interview to the Birmingham Dispatch regarding the plans for the new Institute. Mr A. T. Butler had been appointed the Architect. Mary Macarthur was listed as the Executive Chairman of the Cradley Heath Chainmakers' Association. She said that the grant had been given by the WTUL for the purchase of the site and the erection of a building. The centre, it was hoped, would be used as a centre of social activity, including cinematography shows; Mary Macarthur personally felt that it would be good idea to have a reference library and a bureau of information within the same building. They certainly planned to hold meetings and lectures on the premises and the offices of the local trade unions would be centred there; additionally the trade union offices for the hollowware trades.

The main announcements that she made, were for the locating of the Contributory Unemployed Fund, especially to protect the very old – like Patience – and the infirm. By this stage the union had become acutely aware that the minimum wage and the recession were beginning to have negative effects on the employment of many and some actions now had to be taken. At the same time nationally, Mary Macarthur was chasing after a much bigger prize, the State Insurance Bill – this would be the forerunner to the National Insurance Scheme – this would enable many to receive health care through an insurance scheme for the first time. The National Federation of Women Workers were hoping to become an approved body when the Bill passed into law; and were considering how to distribute the new benefit from the Institute Offices.

The Institute was planned to become the centre of the community, the central hub for all improvement of the mind and body. This centre would provide all the local people access to a world that they had been divorced from through poverty; art, leisure and culture, the things that most never had any time to consider because they were too busy trying to earn money to survive. It was also offering a base for the protection of those that had in some way been harmed by the setting of the minimum rate; at the same time offering opportunity, to re-educate or train many to do other things. Ultimately, it was to become a beacon of the new State system of support for the disadvantaged that was beginning to form in its embryonic stages of development; a place of unemployment benefits, of help with healthcare. Most importantly, although a woman's trade union had fought for women workers, this place was not about women only, it was about the complete community, it was about the rights of all workers.

The County Express (17.6.1911), pictured an artist impression of what the new Institute would look like; it contained a suite of offices and a meeting hall to hold 600 people. There were also plans to have a legal office there; and 'as secretary of the local branch of the National Federation of Women Workers, Mr Charles E. Sitch will have charge of the Institute.'

By the 7th February, 1912, the Wolverhampton Chronicle was reporting that the Institute had been opened by the Countess of Warwick on the Monday previously, the Institute was now running a two-day fund raising bazaar over which, Mr John Fellows was presiding supported by the Countess. There was still money to raise to offset the building costs. Charles Sitch was quoted as saying that 'the new institute would cost £2,600 and £1,500 was granted by the Federation from the funds which were raised to help the women in the recent strike.' He went on to clarify that they hoped to raise £300 from the bazaar, and that through subscriptions they had received £147 and 18s; with a substantial contribution of £75 from the Chainmakers' and Strikers' Association, who had promised a further £25 when the £300 had been raised. The 'Socialistic Countess' as she was referred to by the newspaper, made her delight known:

"The Countess of Warwick said she was delighted to have the opportunity of helping them in the bazaar. She did not feel a stranger amongst them, because she had heard so much of the Cradley Heath women from their friend Mary Macarthur, and they need not look upon her as a stranger. All the country was moved when the women made such a brave fight for their rights, for the rights to live and a living wage. The chainmakers' set the women workers of the country an example and all organised labour had been stirred. It showed that when they linked themselves together they could move mountains, whereas isolated efforts failed. All women owed a debt of gratitude to the chainmakers' for the stand they had made. They had better conditions now, and she hoped they would persevere, so that they would have improved conditions for their children. She believed that was the incentive that had made them make a stand. They all knew she was a socialist – (applause) – and that she did not believe in the wage system at all. The system had to change, and, willingly or not, political people were realizing how fast that change was coming. The workpeople wanted leisure to develop the faculties which had been given to them. In building the Institute they were making a start side by side with the governing classes... she believed that in the near future there would be a great national awakening."

This prediction by the Countess of Warwick was already coming to pass as many around her that day at the bazaar could testify. For the main national organisers of the dispute things had been very busy in the last eighteen months. The Cradley Heath strike had awakened something in the general malaise of all the downtrodden and suppressed around the country; for the first time many believed that they were within their rights to stand up and be heard, that their claims for a fairer working life had to be listened to, and more importantly acted on.

Initially, it had been the process of the other three Trade Boards which had been started by the legislation; J. J. Mallon encountered considerable apathy and depression in the lace workers of Nottingham, as he moved on from Cradley to take on the new challenges. However, Mary Macarthur with her own distinct brand of unionism and her passion for the cause, was there and within a relatively short time a new agreement was made; another minimum wage settled. In his book, Poverty: Yesterday and To-day (1930).

J. J. Mallon was proudly advocating the success of the Trade Boards, this system that he had tirelessly campaigned for, for so long; he sat on many of the Boards, not just the first four. By time of the publication of the book, he was writing that to that date another 37 Trade Boards had been established helping some 1,500,000 working people. Quite an achievement by 1930, however, not fast enough for many who wanted action then, especially as the country was consumed in the grip of a new recession, with the cost of living rising outstripping every rise that they had, this was the time of the 'Great Unrest'.

It could be argued that Cradley Heath coming at the beginning of that period that we have historically identified in those terms was the catalyst, the spark that triggered the general rise to civil dispute across the nation. However, it could also be argued that there was a general feeling of dissatisfaction welling-up in all of the working classes before then and that Cradley Heath was the first dispute that really took hold of the public's attention; as a result of the magnificent publicity campaign. That the strike was seen as a symbol of the beginning of the rise in the workers to be recognised and rewarded fairly, of that there is no doubt.

All across the country the sweated worker began to realise that their plight was not one that could be ignored any longer; particularly the women, who for so long had been at the bottom of the pile, now they knew that they had a 'voice' or access to that voice through the NFWW, and they began to agitate. Other unions too, began to attract large support, particularly the Workers' Union, a union that did not discriminate on the grounds of sex, but viewed all workers as a collective, regardless of their gender. This ideological path was more in tune with the thoughts of Julia Varley, who had been persistent in her views that only through organising together as a unified union could the workers have any real chance of progress. Over the coming years, she would gradually break her associations with the NFWW, preferring to support the activities of the WU. In fact, Barnsby (1989) goes as far as stating it was the work of the women's section of the WU, led by Julia Varley, that set off the industrial unrest in the Black Country in 1911. Certainly, this union did grow substantially from 4,500 in 1910, then throughout the period of the 'Great Unrest' to 150,000; and certainly many more women were organised in the Black Country in the WU than the NFWW during that time.

In 1911 the Black Country became a powder keg of industrial unrest, that was sparked by one particular incident, as Barnsby (1998) reports:

"Early in 1911 a branch of the Workers' Union was opened in Bilston. It was joined by workers at John Fellows. Two months later the shop steward was sacked and other members ordered to leave the union. They refused to abandon the union and were then locked out. The numbers involved seemed small – 15 men and 50 women, but the dispute was long and bitter. The police were called in to intimidate the trade unionists and they were arrested en masse as 'disorderly persons'. Fifty summonses were issued and fines imposed. Fifteen, who refused to pay the fines, went to jail. The collaboration of the police with intransigent employers was deplored. Local campaigns were organised to support the workers and pay the fines. What was remarkable to contemporaries was the solidarity of the women. The management brought strike breakers into the factory and the dispute continued for six months. After, this period it was necessary for the Union to admit defeat. But the nightly propaganda in Bilston had served a wider purpose of publicising the union's policy of the minimum wage. Organisation was set up in other factories in the town and a 22/-d minimum conceded in some of them."

This was very much the pattern of the unrest nationally, whether it was large organisations such as the Railway Workers, or smaller incidents such as the one in Bilston, even if the unions failed, it would spark more unrest in neighbouring places and factories. The workers had got the fire within them to want to fight, to seek better remunerations for their work.

The NFWW was always going to have geographical allegiances to London, despite their significant victory in the Black Country, after all they were a London-centric organisation, with the Head Office and the leaders based there. However, this dissatisfaction was national, and no more acutely felt than in the nation's capital. Mary Macarthur and her colleagues very much had their hands full that August in 1911. It all happened one very warm summer morning, when quite literally, because of the transport strikes nothing was moving; the East End of London could finally take no more, and took to the streets. Mary Agnes Hamilton (1925) describes what occurred that morning:

"One morning in August the women in a big confectionery factory suddenly left work: came out in a body and marched down the street. From factory and workshop as they passed the workers came out and joined them as though the Pied Piper was calling. The doors of great jam, biscuit and food preparation factories, of workshops where girls were making sweet stuff, glue or tin boxes, of tea packing houses and perambulator works opened and gave forth their contingents, to swell the singing, laughing procession."

One can only begin to imagine, the dense odour that these factories produced normally, but remembering that summer had been particularly warm, the air and the conditions of work must have been putrid, which is why so many were employed there. When the NFWW arrived on the scene in Bermondsey to take control of the situation, thousands of women had simply walked out of their factories in outright rebellion, none organised in the trade unions; the NFWW had a mammoth task ahead of them, thousands were enrolled to the Federation in one day alone. The enrolment into the union proved a daunting task in itself, as many of the women had never washed in their lives, which added to the already strong, sickening, smell that pervaded the area.

Just as with Cradley Heath, Mary Macarthur took all that she was confronted with in her stride; appealing this time for bread to feed the workers rather than money. Her team went into factory after factory, to negotiate for their members; by the end of the three weeks of the disputes according to Hamilton (1925) 'advances had been granted in eighteen out of the twenty-one strikes', an astonishing collective increase of £7,000 per year.

This pattern of disruption and industrial action continued unabated with the various unions having to fight for the rights of the individuals concerned Thom (1998) argues that it was driven primarily through the dissatisfaction of the women workers:

"The industrial unrest of the years 1907-14 has been described by historians as the 'great unrest'. In parts of the country it was in fact unrest among women, for example in London and the Black Country. Women did join unions in greater numbers than before, they went on strikes more frequently… There were specifically female characteristics to the unrest. Women were more likely to take strike action, they used suffrage tactics of propaganda and demonstration, and produced many leaflets, songs, postcards, ribbons and badges to publicise their struggles."

By that same token, it could be argued that this was the whole mood and tempo that came about as a consequence of the Cradley Heath strike, which had gained some workers a comprehensive victory; and combined with one of the most influential union leaders – Mary Macarthur, it was perceived by many women as a way to achieve victory themselves. There is little wonder that these strikes driven by mainly women workers were located in these two areas of the country; London with the NFWW centring its core activities there abetted by Macarthur's leadership, and the Black Country, where Julia Varley was based and who was seen as instrumental by many local women in Cradley Heath; and continued to have significant influence via the Workers' Union. In fact, Thom (1998) credits her activities in the Black Country leading to a 'surge in activity' in the engineering shops. That is not to say that the paths of these two unions did not cross throughout this period, for there were still agitations in Lye and Cradley Heath that brought the NFWW back to fight again, this time for the hollowware workers.

The women employed there were working in even more appalling conditions than their fellow women workers had in the chainmaking industry; they were employed in the manufacture and enamelling of metal items. They too worked for 1d an hour, but suffered many associated health risks; breathing difficulties and poisoning, but despite all of these risks continued to carry on because it was the only work they could get and the only way they could feed themselves. They were happy to settle for 10s per week because that would make their lives significantly better; quite an astounding thought when we consider that eighteen months previously the chainmakers had settled for 1s more. However, as Hutchins (1915) points out the case these women put to the unions was so drastic, and so necessary, the union felt compelled to support them in these efforts:

"As a result of conferences between representatives of the National Federation of Women Workers and twenty of the principal employers, during the summer of 1912, it was decided to demand a minimum wage of 10s. for a fifty-four-hour week. Not, of course, that the officials considered this a fair or adequate wage, but because it was hoped it would give the women a starting point from which they could advance in the future, and because, wretched as it seemed, it did in fact represent a considerable increase for some of the women."

This is why when the 'Stute' as the Institute became known locally, opened in early 1912 it was also dedicated to serving the interests of the hollowware workers.

By June 1913, many disputes had arisen nationally and many had been settled successfully; by far the most active unions had been those few women's unions, whose much smaller operations had meant a very intensive workload through that time, whereas the male trade unions had larger logistical powers at their disposal. Equally, it could be argued that the women's agitation tended to be settled favourably for several reasons; firstly, they had never been paid that significantly, so what they were asking for could in the most instances be absorbed in manufacturing costs; secondly, they used the well-worn tactics of Cradley that were non-violent and non-confrontational, they gained support rather than condemnation; thirdly, because of the charisma and experience possessed by the women who led these groups of organised women, which in turn galvanised all around them into positive action.

The 'great unrest' only came to a halt because of circumstances, not because the winds of change had blown through; the advent of WW1 turned everyone's attentions – rich and poor alike – to a more important threat. As in the past with so many other conflicts, at a time of war collective agitation would stop and it did. However, that period did bring some remarkable outcomes for the Black Country as Barnsby (1998) concludes:

"Thus ended arguably the most important episode in Black Country labour history. The effect of raising wages from 18/-d to 23/-d is difficult to overestimate. Not only did it lift perhaps one third of all the Black Country families from a life of perpetual penury to one in which they at least could purchase the main necessities of life, but the social effects of having some control over their lives and the lives of their families brought new attitudes of confidence and self respect."

By July 1913, the National Federation of Women Workers were able to hold their 6th Annual Conference at the Cradley Heath Workers Institute, once again drawing the public's attention to the little town in the Black Country. This event is recorded in the Wolverhampton Express and Star (13.7.1913) and the NFWW issued a statement commenting that:

"Patient work is being done towards the emancipation of sweated workers in Black Country."

A much changed town, full of optimism and colour; a place where women found themselves believing in a future for them and their children. The NFWW Conference report was able to announce that their membership had now gone from 10,000 to 15,000 members and they had expanded their branches from 48 to 74. On the agenda were items such as; fines and deductions still an issue, and how the sweater would often avoid paying full rates; also the National Insurance Scheme, the opportunity for women to access decent medical care for the first time. A system that the NFWW would find themselves hard-pressed to deliver, once the claims started to come in, because no one had ever really researched the plight of women and the effects of child birth on the body. Eventually, costs to the state would have to be dramatically revised upwards as the true effects of poverty were visible through how much the scheme was used.

However, all was not quite sweetness and light for the women chainmakers of Cradley Heath. They had approached the Trade Board again in 1913 for a modest raise in the rate from 2½d per hour to 2¾d; obviously times were hard again with the rising cost of living due to the inflation which had gripped the country. The Trade Board were reluctant to settle, but did eventually. Unfortunately, prosecution after prosecution then ensued against those employers refusing to pay the new rate.

So, this is how life continued for a long time after the Great War and to WW2; the supreme advance for women coming with the securing of the right to vote during that time. After having been excluded from any rights for so long, they were finally recognised, in law anyway, as being equal members of society. This would take a considerably longer period of time to filter into the culture of society as an accepted fact and practice; much of this was due to the deference of women, particularly amongst the working class, to make themselves subordinate to all other groups. That was generational, and would take generations to work itself through, as women had been enshrined as the underclass a hundred years previously, so this would be a long process of re-education.

The chainmaking industry was a relic of its time. Once the inevitable mechanisation swept the world, the local industry suffered not just because of the local employers adapting to new methods, but because of many other foreign competitors making chain at substantially lower costs. Cradley Heath lost its traditional place as where all chain was made. Like the death of the industry, so the chainmakers themselves became like the dinosaur, facing extinction; an oddity, a local curiosity.

It was to some extent amazing that it survived as long as it did, into the 1970's; still anecdotal stories from the 1960's of a thriving back-street workshop industry continuing at the back of the houses; as it always had done. Why had it survived that long? Simply because those chainmakers still left were the women; those on the cheapest rates, who would work for less, and probably got an enormous sense of satisfaction for the work that they did. Moss (1977) shares such stories with us, that paint a picture of a life that had changed little:

"A similar story was told to me by the 'gaffer' of a local chain works, still in business, that they had a woman chainmaker working on their top hearth near the gates who, although she never mentioned it (a lot of Black Country people kept themselves to themselves), was obviously pregnant or 'expectin'. Without warning one day she wasn't seen at the hearth 'mekin the sparks fly' but she was there on time the next morning with her few hours old baby in a basket near the warmth of the fire.

Similar stories like this had been relayed to me before. A gentleman who lives close to me 'broke the record', he informed me. His mother who worked all hours making chain in Old Hill worked one day 6am to 6pm, then went home to have her baby and returned well wrapped up to continue making chain at 10pm. She died in 1969 aged 74! I have been told recently that her mother was making chain in the same chainshops at the age of 93!'

These strong women, were a breed apart and continued to work the forges until the very last days. One particular lady became quite a local celebrity as one of the last of the chainmakers. Her name was Lucy Woodall, and she was reported to still have been working at her forge when she was 71, back in 1970. "Lucy the Chain" as she was known even gained the title of the last of the chainmakers, as she retired from the work in 1973 when her arthritis made it impossible for her to continue. From what has been written about her, it sounds like times never got any better for the domestic workers; certainly the wages seemed to have got worse, as she recounts earning only 9s a week at her peak. She had been advised by her school to go into dressmaking, but was determined to follow her mother and generations of female relatives and her reply to her school superintendent had been "No, miss, I am going into chains." Indeed, that is what she had done for forty-eight years; the same conditions following a two-year apprenticeship that every women had faced. The same injurious occupation, the same hardships; even losing her husband – a collier – early to pneumonia. Why did she choose such a hard labour over a much easier occupation? Her answer was a simple one, it was the companionship; the camaraderie of the workers, working in the forges, she liked it!

When the industry finally did die with the death of Lucy Woodall, it became a museum piece at the Black Country Living Museum. This is where you will find a very nice young lady, demonstrating the process to all the visitors; not with iron anymore but with steel. But it is thanks to that museum that so much of what happened in 1910 is being kept alive for posterity, visitors can actually walk into the 'The Stute' taken down brick-by-brick and carefully reassembled in a prime position. Once a year, the TUC gather to celebrate the past with the Chainmakers' Festival, to the TUC it is a symbol of all that they stand for, and all they continue to fight for; the right of every man and woman to a living wage.

Chapter 12

CONCLUSIONS

"Fight the wrong that needs resistance,
For the future in the distance,
And the good that you can do."

(Mary Reid Macarthur, 1910)

This quotation was given by Thomas Sitch on the foundation of the 'Workers' Institute' and attributed to Macarthur's first visit to Cradley Heath, it was used as the inspirational message to all who used the 'Stute'. There is no doubt that Mary Macarthur has been remembered as the most significant figure of the dispute, but I have argued that it is by virtue of the changing face of social intervention and the writing and recording of history. That is not to say that she was not the catalyst for much of the action, or even without her that there would have been a successful outcome, because I do not believe that to be the case.

Mary Macarthur was an extraordinarily, dynamic woman, and if we consider her age and the wealth of experience that she had gained in such a relatively short time, it is not hard to see that she was incredibly competent and driven. It was that determination that made her into the great union activist that she has been acclaimed for. She had a 'modern' approach to promoting a cause; using the press, and image to great advantage. She exploited many of the suffragette tactics for delivering a message, and undertaking peaceful protest, though she was far removed from that politics and disavowed feminism. Her main principle for undertaking any cause, was to see the disadvantage of the female worker rectified, and only to take action if it could be successfully achieved. She believed in the right to a living wage, a political aim of many, especially the more sophisticated London-based, social-interest groups.

Edwardian society was driven by a desire to correct social injustice, by all probability because the emergent middle class had experienced a certain amount of those injustices, as they progressed in society. Not that their perceived social injustices could, in any way, be comparable with the level that the working class were exposed to through the 'sweated work system' of exploitative practice and disinterest; but the awakening middle class consciousness, was of the opinion that society needed to be rebalanced to create greater equity and equality; they considered that it was their mission to correct the wrongs that had been done.

It can be argued that many of these social causes were misplaced, and in the interests of the middle class conscience and not always in the best interests of those they sought to serve. Thom (1998) argues that although much good was done, not all things were considered, for instance, the cause of the sweated worker quite rightly needed addressing, however, was it in the interests of the sweated worker whose income was threatened? This was the point that Margaret MacDonald sought to highlight in her campaign not to set minimum wages and seek the Trade Boards Act; she regarded this as more detrimental for those who depended on their only source of income, as low as it was, for any increase in costs would make them unemployable.

There is a tipping point, where a decision to follow a path has to be taken and when the general consensus is in one direction, then ultimately for the greater good of many, it must be pursued at the expense of those very few. The National Anti-Sweating League, led the vanguard to expose the inhumanities of the system and the challenge went out to every person in the land to take their own social responsibility for the lives of the exploited working classes. If we read the claims made in certain texts, Mary Macarthur was as great an influence in the establishment of the NASL, as she was in the NFWW, and the Cradley Heath dispute. However, as I have argued in previous texts (Debney 2006, Debney 2010), any reading or writing of history is a purely subjective judgment and as such open to many interpretations.

The rise of the media coincided with much of this particular age of social history, consequently the powerful use of image and story at that time has had a large impact on how we view those events today. The volume of evidence that was channelled through the London Press and to some extent the provincial press can slant those views to a more sensationalist analysis of the actual facts. There is no doubt that the imagery used, pictures of the women, even cinematography images, for the most part project one particular view. Thom (1998) argues that working class women as the sweated worker became a paradigm frozen in time a 'symbol of the unacceptable present', which brought pressure to bear for policy and legislation. Much of the images of the Cradley Heath women with their chains set this course in motion; however, were they the sweated unskilled worker as portrayed? Or as they tried to argue a skilled exploited workforce?

As Thom (1998) stresses, this misuse of image created a false perception in the minds of many, that all women's work was less than:

"The image was no longer that <u>some</u> women worked because they were poor and unsupported. It was one in which <u>all</u> women's labour was that of the weak and defenceless."

Working class women, worked because they had to, there was simply not enough income from any wage, whether male or female, to support a family. However, women's wages were indisputably lower than men's, and this has to be as a consequence of their lowest role in society; as women in the lower class, and as all women without rights of recognition. Consequently, it meant that nothing that they did could be regulated or controlled, it exposed them to the dangers of exploitation by those without conscience and the women were viewed by unions as a threat to the established male trades because of their position to undercut wages. This exposed them to further pressures from their own families and communities and from the closed trade unions who refused to accept their admittance. As the women could not be regulated, they could not be protected through organisation either; it became a vicious circle, that increased the spiral downward into poverty.

As society became more industrialised, the poor became poorer; women became the poorest of all, but had to earn a living, doing what they could to survive, hence the perpetuation of sweating. As I have endeavoured to outline in this book there were many sweated trades and all very heavily exploitative, but it is easy to argue that card board box making, does not carry the same cache, or create such a powerful an image, as Patience Round, 79 years old, carrying her chains. I am sure when Mary Macarthur and the NFWW, considered their tactics that might be employed to raise the public's attention to the cause of the minimum wage, the Cradley Heath chainmakers projected the greatest opportunities for attention-grabbing, despite the argument that the chainmakers were skilled and not as most sweated trades, unskilled. The dispute was a public relations coup which created so much interest, that it set the pattern for the continuing minimum wage settling, but in the process established certain iconographic images and personalities into our historical view.

I have endeavoured to create an overlying picture in this book of all the other forces and interests in this work, to try to re-establish a balance to that perspective. I have consistently argued that many forces and triggers were coalescing at one and the same time, both nationally and locally, which all came together in a confluence of activity, which neither commenced or concluded with the Cradley Heath victory. The culmination of the Cradley Heath strike, provides us with a fixed period in history to work to, or from, because we need a focal point to chart the social progress against. The dispute, sits against the backdrop of the social philanthropic wave of interest groups culminating in the NASL; the rise in women's organisation with the establishment of the NFWW; the commencement of the period that we identify as the 'great unrest', however, that does not mean that it was point of arrival or departure, it is just an event in that time frame, but an incredibly significant one.

The settling of the minimum wage was by no doubt a great achievement that significantly changed the lives of many, however, it was part of a general progress of legislation that led to a more equal society, along with the Old Age Pensions Act 1908 and the National Insurance Act 1911. These actions were both driven by the demands of the public and the determination of the more socially active in Government; Sir Charles Dilke, David Lloyd George and Ramsay MacDonald to name but a very few. Additionally, we must consider their associated friends and family who created the groundswell of interest, who to some extent have also been obscured by the sensational publicity of the time, we must not forget; Lady Emilia Dilke, Clementina Black, Margaret MacDonald, Julia Varley and Gertrude Tuckwell, who fall into the shadows of Mary Macarthur, yet were as instrumental in all of this.

Mary Macarthur, was young and pretty, she was clever and determined, she understood journalism and knew how to exploit a story to gain maximum advantage (Thom 1998). She had incredible skills to organise women, with her oratory and presence. When the stories were printed in her friendly newspapers, she became the face of the dispute, and to a larger extent the voice. Would the Cradley Heath strike have been as successful without her? Would the dispute have happened at all? Those are both questions that are difficult to answer, for without knowing whether there would have been another with all of those necessary skills, to marshal all of the forces together, it is impossible to guess. Or indeed, whether the dispute arising was to some extent driven by the involvement of the NFWW? As indeed it appears that it may have been, as there had been significant interest in the Cradley Heath chainmakers years before by the WTUL, and the organisation by the NFWW in Cradley Heath commenced at the same time as the activities of the NASL. We have to remember that for years the women of that town had been unable to organise and had to some extent accepted that they were unable to change their situation; they were inspired to do so by Mary Macarthur.

If there had not been a Liberal Government in power in 1906 with the aid of their small band of Labour coalition partners would so much have been achieved in such a short time? Undoubtedly not, for the alternative was an old regime of inaction and inactivity, but the more that was given the more that was needed, the actions when they came were not fast enough. The UK was already an ailing economy in recession yet again, wages were low, but inflation was spiralling making any wage substantially lower. Cradley Heath was a symbol to many oppressed and tired workers across the land.

As the dispute became settled, it gave hope to thousands that they too, could be recognised and paid a living wage; and the Government was – as it appeared – on their side. It is significant that the increase in industrial unrest seemed to grow substantially post-Cradley Heath, but I believe that is as much a part of the rise in the dissatisfaction of the working class in general to fight their injustices, as any stimulation of the chainmakers' strike. For the minimum wage settled was difficult to enforce then, and in the intervening years before WW1 with the increase awarded; many court cases against employers who refused to settle are recorded. I argue here, that the settlement of that wage was as much a symbol of hope to the local people of Cradley Heath as their dispute was to the country as a whole.

Even without the proper and fair wage settlement, to which we know Mary Macarthur and Thomas Sitch capitulated, they wanted to settle for a larger amount – and subsequently the rise was outstripped by inflation and to some extent unenforceable – the townsfolk of Cradley Heath were invigorated with their victory. It brought a sense of pride to the community, it gave a recognition to a town that had become a 'black spot' in many hearts and minds. It was noted that people dressed better – not necessarily newer clothes – but better presented generally. The town took heart in their new 'Stute' which became a focal point to remember what they had fought for; it brought new opportunities to their lives.

No more were they the 'down trodden' of the Black Country, as much as the Black Country was overshadowed by its more affluent neighbour – Birmingham; Cradley Heath achieved a cultural identity that could not be overwritten by history. As Birmingham had risen under its powerful guru Joseph Chamberlain and become a bastion of Liberalism and to some extent eventually lost its way for a short while with his eventual downfall and demise; so the Black Country, always a hotbed of radicalism – found its political voice in the rise of socialism and the loss of the Liberal Caucus grip on the region. As with the outcome of that strike, that political ascendancy of socialism, was more of a psychological uprising in the people than a promotion of any identifiable materialistic status.

The national mass movement for change which had started in the middle-class consciousness – whether motivations were misguided or not – swept through the creation of policy and legislation. The wave of optimism became manifest in the general dissatisfaction of those that had been historically oppressed and like the stone in the pond, the ripples were magnified across the land, till every industry or trade felt the effects of those on less, demanding more. All was halted with the advent of WW1, a national respect, or jingoism, stopped that wave, but it was not going to go away completely. Despite the fact that mass unemployment came with war, followed by wages being outstripped by rip-roaring inflation and a new form of sweated labour emerged with women diluted to make munitions; post war finally brought the long awaited restoration of the franchise to women. From there, there was indeed progress, once the vote was given to women and they were able to make their mark and become part of that voting population to be respected; they became a force to be reckoned with. Further, once Mary Macarthur's long time friend, Margaret Bondfield, took her place in Ramsay MacDonald's Cabinet, women were finally being restored as people.

What many predicted with the advent of the minimum wage – Margaret MacDonald in particular – the death of some trades rendering many unemployed, did occur; many viewed this as a necessary casualty of the process of change, the workers themselves simply lost their livelihoods and had to start again, there was very little social philanthropy for them. Eventually, Cradley Heath felt the effects of that death of a trade which could be done cheaper elsewhere, or by machine, and chainmaking died out. It was never truly a sweated trade, it was a skilled occupation that was extremely badly paid. As the chainmakers left or died, their skills went too, as has happened in so many traditional occupations. I myself trained in glass in Stourbridge, once the centre for the whole country in glassmaking, now gone, as with many of the industries which kept the Black Country working, all now are museum pieces, oddities from a bygone age.

I am writing this conclusion during the week of the 2010 General Election, when as predicted our political map changed to a coalition of government, due to a hung Parliament. I wonder what our future holds, especially as we sit reflecting on the worst recession that has existed in living memory? They say, that for the solutions to the problems, we should look to history for the answers. It seems that history has come full-circle and returned to a similar experience of the one in 1910, the distinct difference being that most of the manufacturing industry that made both Birmingham and the Black Country has long since gone, it has even left the shores of the UK. The people still remain, the hardworking and determined people, that made these places what they are, that developed the cultural identities that are very much associated to these areas; our funny accents and words. Then there is Cadbury's, once such an institution to the country, certainly of greatest significance to the Birmingham people. The family that lived and breathed social justice and even built their business empire upon that; what would Edward Cadbury say now if he could be here knowing that Cadbury's is no longer British, no longer Brummie?

If you visit the Black Country Living Museum, make your way down the hill past the pit yard and before you get to the streets, on your left, you will see the 'Stute' rebuilt in all of its glory. Go in there and imagine yourself at a meeting of the NFWW in 1913 and Mary Macarthur has come to speak. Stand at the stage and listen to her inspirational words, and hear all of the others around you, electrified, and full of hope; hope that had been born of success. Then make your way over the bridge to the chainmakers' house and watch the girl making the chain; try to imagine a very long day, children dangerously close to the hot forge, no food to be eaten till mother stops; and the prospect of very little money at the end of the week. That was what Cradley Heath was all about, not chains, not strikes, not unions or socialism, it was about giving hope to the hopeless, giving a chance to live a life, and with the victory achieved by the women chainmakers' strike of 1910, that is what it succeeded in doing for millions just like them.

THE SONG OF THE SHIRT
– THOMAS HOOD

With fingers weary and worn,
With eyelids heavy and red,
A woman sat, in unworthy rags,
Plying her needle and thread –
Stitch! stitch! stitch!
In poverty, hunger and dirt,
And still with a voice of dolorous pitch
She sang the 'Song of the shirt.'

'Work! work! work!
While the cock is crowing aloof!
And work – work – work,
Till the stars shine through the roof!
It's Oh! to be a slave
Along with the barbarous Turk,
Where woman has never a soul to save,
If this is Christian work!

'Work – work – work!
Till the brain begins to swim;
Work – work – work
Till the eyes are heavy and dim!
Seam, and gusset, and band,
Band, and gusset, and seam,
Till over the buttons I fall asleep,
And sew them on in a dream!

'Oh, Men, With Sisters dear!
Oh, Men, with Mothers and Wives!

It is not linen you're wearing out,
But human creatures' lives!
Stitch – stitch – stitch,
In poverty, hunger and dirt,
Sewing at once, with a double thread,
A shroud as well as a shirt.

'But why do I talk of death?
That phantom of grisly bone,
I fear his terrible shape,
It seems so like my own –
It seems so like my own,
Because of the fasts I keep;
Oh, God! That bread should be so dear,
And flesh and blood so cheap!

'Work – work – work!
My labour never flags;
And what are its wages? A bed of straw,
A crust of bread – and rags,
That shattered roof – and this naked floor –
A table – a broken chair –
And a wall so blank, my shadow I thank
For sometimes falling there!

'Work – work – work!
From weary chime to chime,
Work – work – work –
As prisoners work for crime!
Band, and gusset, and seam,
Seam, and gusset, and band,
Till the heart is sick, and the brain benumb'd,
As well as the weary hand.

'Work – work – work!
In the dull December light,
And work – work – work,
When the weather is warm and bright –
While underneath the eaves

The brooding swallows cling
As if to show me their sunny backs
And twit me with the spring.

'Oh! but to breathe the breath
Of the cowslip and primrose sweet –
With the sky above my head,
And the grass beneath my feet,
For only one short hour
To feel as I used to feel,
Before I knew the woes of want
And the walk that costs a meal!

'Oh but for one short hour
A respite however brief!
No blessed leisure for Love or Hope,
But only time for Grief!
A little weeping would ease my heart,
But in their briny bed
My tears must stop, for every drop
Hinders needle and thread!

With fingers weary and worn,
With eyelids heavy and red
A woman sat in unwomanly rags,
Plying her needle and thread –
Stitch! stitch! stitch!
In poverty, hunger, and dirt,
And still with a voice of dolorous pitch –
Would that its tone could reach the Rich! –
She sang this 'Song of the Shirt!'

Appendix II

REBECCA, STORIES OF CHAIN MAKING – YVONNE ROUTLEDGE

The following anecdotes were passed down to me by my mother Sadie and my grandmother Edith. They are oral recollections, but some have been supported by documents I have read outlining conditions for chain makers in the Cradley area from late 1800s to early 1900s.

Rebecca Siviter (nee Tromans), my great grandmother was born in 1869, the daughter of John and Hannah Tromans. The 1901 census records Hannah as a chain maker and John as a chain manufacturer. I understand from my mother and grandmother that John and Hannah were poor but not in poverty. They had approx 12 children and Rebecca was either the eldest or one of the eldest. Rebecca had little formal education; even as an adult she had difficulty in reading. I suspect that at an early age she was required to help with raising her younger siblings.

Rebecca married Samuel Siviter, a chain maker, and they rented a house in Brook Lane. I remember this house well; it had 2 small rooms downstairs and 2 bedrooms upstairs. There was no garden front or back but it did have a wash house in a cobbled yard at the rear, called by Black Country people "the fode" I think the wash house contained a tin bath and a copper for doing the family washing. The house was a row or terraced house and may have shared an outside toilet with other houses in the row. These houses have since been demolished. Although the house in Brook Lane was spartan it was much better that many of the back to back houses shown in the Black Country museum.

During the early years of marriage Rebecca was supported by Samuel and may not have needed to work. They had three children Edith (my grandmother), Leonard and John. When Edith was four, Leonard approx two and John six months their father Samuel died.

Edith described that there was no social welfare and her mother had to go before a Parish Board to ask for assistance. It was humiliating for her to ask a group of strange and relatively prosperous men for help. The Board were mainly stern and stated that Rebecca was healthy and could work. One man was described as kind pointing out that one of her children was only six months and not yet weaned. As a result she received some minor assistance; I believe 6 pence per week until John was weaned. Edith described that when she first attended school she did not have to pay the penny per week because her mother was receiving assistance but she did have to have pauper embroidered on her school apron.

Six pence was clearly not enough to keep the family so Rebecca became a chain maker and she is recorded as this in the 1901 census. Edith told us that her young brother John died from burns after falling in the fire. Initially we imagined an accident in a domestic fireplace but after reading I am inclined to think it happened at the open forge whilst Rebecca was working. As a toddler John would have been particularly vulnerable to this type of accident.

I am not sure if Rebecca was involved in the strike of 1910 although this is likely and it certainly seems that one of her sisters, possibly Prudence Tromans, was involved. Edith recalled that one of her aunts was quite radical and went on to be involved in some way with the suffragettes. I suspect that she was one of the strikers signed up by Mary MacArthur (sic) to be involved in the suffragette movement after the strike. Edith stated that she thought that her aunt joined the Jarrow marchers on their march to London and marched with chains around her neck.

Family stories suggest that Rebecca's financial position improved. Her brother John started a bakery in Brook Lane which seemed to be quite successful. He may have helped Rebecca financially or at least with free bread supplies. Also Rebecca took on some sort of role as a local midwife. Apparently the local doctor was an alcoholic who was frequently too drunk to attend births. Rebecca delivered many local babies and we understand that she continued to do this into her seventies. She may have attempted some type of formal certificate because it was mentioned that she attended the Institute library to practise reading. However it is more likely that she was paid informally and supplemented her income as a chain maker.

Edith certainly worked as a chain maker for some period but she also learned dress making. She married Joseph Hill and they had one surviving child, my mother Sadie. I believe that Edith and Joseph did not marry until well after my mother's birth in 1911. Joseph had migrated to America and after a few years wanted Edith and Sadie to join him. Rebecca persuaded her not to go so Joseph returned, married Edith and they lived with Rebecca until after the end of world war one. I do not think this was entirely a happy arrangement; Rebecca was fairly dominating which did not suit my grandfather Joseph. After the war Joseph and Edith were able to rent a new council house at number 11, Taylor Road Netherton. I remember many happy hours spent at this house during my childhood. Edith's brother Leonard never married and continued to live in the Brook Lane house after Rebecca died.

My mother Sadie remembered her grandmother Rebecca and her great grandparents Hannah and John well. I believe Hannah and John lived into their early 80s. My mother married William Poulton and in 1945 he stood as labour councillor for south ward in the Dudley council area. Sadie and William had bought their own house in Cradley road in the 1930s. I understand that 1945 was the first time that Rebecca voted labour, persuaded by my father. She had previously voted for Lloyd George's party because he had given votes to women. All the women in my family stressed the importance of voting because of the struggle to get women the vote in the first place. We were a politically active family and spent many hours at Dad's elections posting material and canvassing door to door. At the last election he fought he received 96% of the vote. My father was Mayor of Dudley from 1963 to 1964 and deputy mayor when he died suddenly of a heart attack in late 1964.

My sisters who were 11 and 16 years older than me would remember Rebecca more clearly. Unfortunately they have both died but I have one clear memory, probably around 1954, which was approximately when she died. My mother took me to visit her at the Brook lane house and she was upstairs in bed, probably suffering from her final illness. My mother lifted me onto the bed so that Rebecca could hold me, I was most struck by her hair which was brushed down, long and white. She was well into her 80s when she died.

My grandmother Edith described chain shops as hell holes, black with dirt, dust and soot along with fire and sparks. However she did express some pride in the work that female chain makers achieved. She mentioned that Rebecca had fine fingers and great dexterity and was able to make fine chain. Despite this she was very pleased that I was able to avoid any type of factory work, take advantage of a good education and progress to the extent of my abilities.

Edith and Sadie spent the last years of their lives living in a part of my house in Adelaide. They died within a day of each other in 1993. Edith was 101 and Sadie was 81.

Appendix III

THE HOME-LIFE OF THE SWEATED – GEORGE HAW

An extract from – 'Sweated Industries' A handbook of the 'Daily News' Exhibition – edited by Richard Mudie-Smith
The Home-Life of the Sweated – George Haw

Down by the river at Shadwell, there came to the Boy's Club one night a little fellow with the plea, Would someone come and see his brother?

"It's his consumption," said the little chap. "His cough's that bad, mother says he ain't fit to get up."

Two of us undertook to go. The boy led us across Ratcliff Highway and down a dark street, where, in crossing the swing bridge across the Dock Entrance, we caught a glimpse of the river lights by Limehouse Reach.

"This is it," said the lad, turning into a street where the buildings rose higher than usual, and looked colder and more repelling.

He led the way into a block of tenements. The only light in the passage that opened on the street was that which streamed under the doors on either side.

"Up the stairs," he said, as we stumbled across the bottom one at the end of the passage.

The staircase was densely dark and rickety. There was another close and dark passage on the first floor, with streams of light swelling under the doors in the same way as seen below.

The boy opened a door. We recoiled. Such a strong odour as arose wellnigh came over us. Through an atmosphere of floating fluff we saw a woman engaged in fur-pulling. Two young children were sleeping on a bed with rabbit skins strewn about on the coverings.

"Shut the door, for God's sake!" cried the woman, as the draught set the throat sticking substance in a whirl. "I guess it's the others you've come to see, and not the likes o' me. Never a visit do I get from any one; and my youngest been dead a matter o' seven days, and me a-slaving on from morn till night a-trying to get enough scraped together for the funeral."

136

Putting down her work for a moment, she added in a softer tone, "Just look at her; she ain't changed much."

The woman went to the bed on which two children were sleeping, and tossing aside a heap of rabbit skins at the foot, she cautiously raised the clothes and revealed the shrunken form of a dead child.

She put the back of her hand to the cold cheek and said the neighbours used to say Alice was always a lovely child.

"But there – don't stay," cried the woman, dropping the clothes over the body. "He hears you behind there. Listen how he's a-coughing."

She nodded to a sheet of dirty sacking suspended by a cord right across the room. Above this sacking the flicker of another light threw varying shadows on the ceiling. The sound of coughing told of someone beyond.

The boy had gone on the other side while the woman talked to us, and he now put his head round the hanging and beckoned us forward.

Another woman, hard at work with a sack in her hand, sat at the head of a bed watching her sick son.

"Ain't coming anymore," said the ailing lad, raising himself a little as we appeared. "Can't."

Then came another fit of coughing.

We suggested the hospital, both mother and son readily consenting. The woman had not ceased plying her needle all the time. We whispered questions about the neighbour sharing her room, the dead baby, and why it was not buried.

The sack-maker raised her head and spoke low, that the other woman might not hear. "Them funeral men won't coffin the body until they get the money down. She's been working day and night almost in order to earn enough, but I reckon she'll have to pawn her wedding ring a'fore she can do it."

"What did the child die of?"

"Don't know. It was took queer one afternoon and she asked me to run for the doctor. The doctor, not knowing her, said he couldn't come unless we brought the money first. So I ran back; and we collected half-a-crown on our landing. But her child died before I could get the doctor with the money."

The consumptive lad and the dead baby were removed from the one-roomed house two days later. Although one went to the hospital first, the same cemetery soon saw them both.

And with two fewer mouths to feed, the fur-puller and the sack-maker went on working as usual in the stuffy room by candle-light, one on each side of the sheet of sacking.

Appendix IV

SONGS FROM THE CRADLEY HEATH CHAINMAKERS' STRIKE OF 1910

Song: "Raise, ye women!"
Tune: Men of Harlech.

Raise, ye women, long enduring.
Beat no Iron, blow no bellows,
Till ye win the fight, ensuring,
Pay that is your due
      Chorus
Through the years uncomplaining
Hope and strength were waning –
       Your industry
       A beggar's fee
A meagre fare was gaining
Now a Trade Board is created
See your pains and death abated
And the sweater's wiles checkmated
Parliament's decree!

Raise ye women, raise, around you,
Towns and cities cry, "God speed you,"
Raise, shake off the fears that bound you,
Women, raise, be true.
      Chorus
At length the light is breaking
The sweater's throne is shaking,
    Oh, do your part,
    With all your hear
A sweater would in making!
Stand together, strong and splendid,

138

In your Union till you've ended
Tyranny, and with toil blended,
Beauty, Joy and Art.

Song: for the Strikers
Tune: John Brown's Body

Strike! Strike! Strike! A blow for freedom every time,
Cast your chains away from you upon the ground;
Strike! Strike! Strike! A blow for freedom every time,
As you go marching around.

Now come along and join the union,
Don't let us have to ask you twice:
Now come along and join the Union,
All fighting for our price.

Song: for the Strikers
Tune: Yankee Doodle

The Chain Makers came along;
With their fine agreement;
They asked us all to sign our names,
For taking lower payment.

Then the Union came along,
Said – Do you want your price, oh!
We said – we do – they didn't have
To ask the question twice oh!

Appendix V

THE PROCESSION
– JOHN GALSWORTHY

Reproduced below is a chapter from *The Inn of Tranquillity and other Impressions* by John Galsworthy.

VI – The Procession

In one of those corners of our land canopied by the fumes of blind industry, there was, on that day, a lull in the darkness. A fresh wind had split the customary heaven, or roof of hell; was sweeping long drifts of creamy clouds across a blue still pallid with reek. The sun even shone – a sun whose face seemed white and wondering. And under the rare sun all the little town, among it slag heaps and few tall chimneys, had an air of living faster. In those continuous courts and alleys, where women worked, smoke from each little forge rose and dispersed into the wind with strange alacrity; amongst the women, too, there was the same eagerness, for the sunshine had crept in and was making pale all those dark-raftered, sooted ceilings which covered them in, together with their immortal comrades, the small open furnaces. About their work they had been busy since seven o'clock; their feet pressing the leather lungs which fanned the conical heaps of glowing fuel, their hands poking into the glow a thin iron rod till the end could be curved into a fiery hook; snapping with a mallet; threading it with tongs on to the chain; hammering, closing the link and, without a second's pause, thrusting the iron rod again into the glow. And while they worked they chattered, laughed sometimes, now and then sighed. They seems of all ages and all types; from her who looked like a peasant of Provence, broad, brown, and strong, to the weariest white consumptive wisp; from old women of seventy, with straggling grey hair, to fifteen-year-old girls. In the cottage forges there would be but one worker, or two at most; in the shop forges four, or even five, little glowing heaps; four or five of the grimy, pale lung-bellows; and never a moment without a fiery hook about to take its place on the growing chains, never a second when the thin smoke of the forges, and of those lives consuming slowly in front of them, did not escape from out of the dingy, white-washed spaces past the dark rafters, away to freedom.

But there had been in the air that morning something more than the white sunlight. There had been anticipation. And at two o'clock began fulfilment. The forges were stilled, and from court and alley forth came the women. In their ragged working clothes, in their best clothes – so little different; in bonnets, in hats, bareheaded, with babies born and unborn, they swarmed into the high street and formed across it behind the band. A strange, magpie, jay-like flock; black, white, patched with brown and green and blue, shifting, chattering, laughing, seeming unconscious of any purpose. A thousand and more of them, with faces twisted and scored by those myriad deformings which a desperate town-toiling and little food fasten on human visages; yet with hardly a single evil or brutal face. Seemingly it was not easy to be evil or brutal on a wage that scarcely bound soul and body. A thousand and more of the poorest-paid and hardest-worked human beings in the world.

On the pavement alongside this strange, acquiescing assembly of revolt, about to march in protest against the conditions of their lives, stood a young woman without a hat and in poor clothes, but with a sort of beauty in her rough-haired, high-cheek-boned, dark-eyed face. She was not one of them; yet by a stroke of Nature's irony, there was graven on her face alone of all those faces, the true look of rebellion; a haughty almost fierce, uneasy look – an untamed look. On all the other thousand faces, one could see no bitterness, no fierceness, not even enthusiasm; only a half-stolid, half-vivacious patience and eagerness as of children going to a party.

The band played; and they began to march. Laughing, talking, waving flags, trying to keep step; with the same expression slowly coming over every face; the future was not, only the present – this happy present of marching behind the discordance of a brass band; this strange present of crowded movement and laughter in open air.

We others – some dozen accidentals like myself, and the tall, grey-haired lady interested in 'the people' together with those few kind spirits in charge of 'the show' – marched too, a little self-conscious, desiring with a vague military sensation to hold our heads up, but not too much, under the eyes of the curious bystanders. Those – nearly all men – were well-wishers, it was said, though their faces, pale from their own work in shop or furnace, expressed nothing but apathy. They wished well, very dumbly, in the presence of this new thing, as if they found it queer that women should be doing something for themselves; queer and rather dangerous. A few indeed, shuffled along between the column and the little hopeless shops and grimy factory sheds, and one or two accompanied their women, carrying the baby. Now and then there passed us some better-to-do citizen – a housewife, or lawyer's clerk, or ironmonger, with lips pressed rather tightly together and an air of taking no notice of this disturbance of traffic, as though the whole thing were a rather poor joke which they had already heard too often.

So, with laughter and a continual crack of voices our jay-like crew swung on, swaying and stumping in the strange ecstasy of irreflection, happy to be moving, they knew not where, nor greatly why, under the visiting sun, to the sound of murdered music. Whenever the band stopped playing, discipline became tatterdemalion as the very flags and garments; but never once did they lose that look of essential order, as if indeed they knew that, being the worst served creatures in the Christian world, they were the chief guardians of the inherent dignity of man.

Hatless, in the very front row, marched a tall slip of a girl, arrow-straight, and so thin, with dirty fair hair, in a blouse and skirt gaping behind, ever turning her pretty face on its pretty slim neck from side-to-side, so that one could see her blue eyes sweeping here, there, everywhere, with a sort of flower-like wilderness, as if secret embracing of each moment forbade her to let them rest on anything and break this pleasure of just marching. It seemed that in the never-still eyes of that anaemic, happy girl the spirit of our march had elected to enshrine itself and to make thence its little excursions to each ecstatic follower. Just behind her marched a little old woman – a maker of chains, they said, for forty years – whose black slits of eyes were sparkling, who fluttered a bit of ribbon, and reeled with her sense of the exquisite humour of the world. Every now and then she would make a rush at one of her leaders to demonstrate how immoderately glorious was life. And each time she spoke the woman next to her, laden with a heavy baby, went off into squeals of laughter. Behind her, again, marched one who beat time with her head and waved a little bit of her stick intoxicated by this noble music.

For an hour the pageant wound through the dejected street, pursuing neither method nor set route, till it came to a deserted slag-heap, selected for the speech making. Slowly the motley regiment swung into that grim amphitheatre under the pale sunshine; and, as I watched, a strange fancy visited my brain. I seemed to see over every ragged head of those marching women a little yellow flame, a thin, flickering gleam, spiring upward and blown back by the wind. A trick of sunlight, maybe? Or was it that the life in their hearts, the inextinguishable breath of happiness, had for a moment escaped prison, and was fluttering at the pleasure of the breeze?

Silent now, just enjoying the sound of the words thrown down to them, they stood, unimaginably patient, with that happiness of they knew not what gilding the air above them between the patchwork ribands of their poor flags. If they could not tell very much why they had come, nor believe very much that they would gain anything by coming; if their demonstration did not mean to the world quite all that oratory would have them think; if they themselves were but the poorest, humblest, least learned women in the land – for all that, it seemed to me that in all those tattered, wistful figures, so still, so trustful, I was looking on such beauty as I had never beheld. All the elaborated glory of things made, the perfected dreams of aesthetes, the embroideries of romance, seemed as nothing beside this sudden vision of the wild goodness native in humble hearts.

BIBLIOGRAPHY

Books

Addison, Paul. "Churchill, Sir Winston Leonard Spencer (1874–1965)." *Oxford Dictionary of National Biography*. Ed. H. C. G. Matthew and Brian Harrison. Oxford: OUP, 2004. Online ed. Ed. Lawrence Goldman. Oct. 2008. 16 Mar. 2010 <http://www.oxforddnb.com/view/article/32413>.

Barnsby, G. (1989) *Birmingham working people* 1st ed. Wolverhampton: IPS.

Barnsby, G. (1990) *Social conditions in the Black Country 1800-1900* 1st ed. Wolverhampton: IPS.

Barnsby, G. (1993) *The working class movement in the Black Country 1750 to 1867* 1st ed. Wolverhampton: IPS.

Barnsby, G (1998) *Socialism in Birmingham and the Black Country 1850-1939* 1st ed. Wolverhampton: IPS.

Black, C. (1907) *Sweated industry and the minimum wage* 1st ed. London: Duckworth & Co.

Blackburn, S. (1987) Employers and social policy: Black-Country chain-masters, the minimum wage campaign and the Cradley Heath strike of 1910 *Midlands History* Vol. XII pp. 85–102.

Briggs, Asa. "Mallon, James Joseph (1874–1961)." M. C. Curthoys *Oxford Dictionary of National Biography*. Ed. H. C. G. Matthew and Brian Harrison. Oxford: OUP, 2004. Online ed. Ed. Lawrence Goldman. May 2007. 3 Mar. 2010 <http://www.oxforddnb.com/view/article/34846>.

Burnett, J. (1974) *Useful toil* 1st ed. London: Penguin.

Cadbury, E. & Shann, G. (1907) *Sweating* 1st ed. London: Headley Brothers.

Cadbury, E. & Matheson, C. M. (1907) *Women's work and wages – a phase of life in an industrial city* 1st ed. Chicago: Chicago Press.

Davis, John. "Webb, (Martha) Beatrice (1858–1943)." *Oxford Dictionary of National Biography*. Ed. H. C. G. Matthew and Brian Harrison. Oxford: OUP, 2004. Online ed. Ed. Lawrence Goldman. May 2008. 16 Mar. 2010 <http://www.oxforddnb.com/view/article/36799>.

Debney, J. (2006) *Engineered Careers? A study of women engineers in the offshore oil and gas industry.* Ed.D Thesis. British Library. (unpublished).

Debney, J. (2010) *The Dangerfields* 1st ed. Birmingham: Brewin Books.

Doughan, David. "Varley, Julia (1871–1952)." *Oxford Dictionary of National Biography*. Ed. H. C. G. Matthew and Brian Harrison. Oxford: OUP, 2004. 2 Mar. 2010 <http://www.oxforddnb.com/view/article/42094>.

Drake, B. (1917) *Women in the engineering trades* 1st ed. London: Fabian.

Foucault, M. (1998) *The Will to Knowledge: The History of Sexuality. 1.* 1st ed. London: Penguin.

Fraser, Hilary. "Dilke, Emilia Francis, Lady Dilke (1840–1904)." *Oxford Dictionary of National Biography*. Ed. H. C. G. Matthew and Brian Harrison. Oxford: OUP, 2004. Online ed. Ed. Lawrence Goldman. Jan. 2008. 1 Mar. 2010 <http://www.oxforddnb.com/view/article/32825>.

Galsworthy, J. (1912) *The Inn of Tranquillity* 1st ed. London: Heinemann.

Grenier, Janet E. "Black, Clementina Maria (1853–1922)." *Oxford Dictionary of National Biography*. Ed. H. C. G. Matthew and Brian Harrison. Oxford: OUP, 2004. Online ed. Ed. Lawrence Goldman. Oct. 2008. 1 Mar. 2010 <http://www.oxforddnb.com/view/article/37196>.

Hamilton, M. A. (1925) *Mary Macarthur – A biographical sketch* 1st ed. London: Leonard Parsons.

Hannam, June. "MacDonald, Margaret Ethel Gladstone (1870–1911)." *Oxford Dictionary of National Biography*. Ed. H. C. G. Matthew and Brian Harrison. Oxford: OUP, 2004. Online ed. Ed. Lawrence Goldman. Jan. 2008. 1 Mar. 2010 <http://www.oxforddnb.com/view/article/45462>.

Harborough Sherard, R. (1898) *The white slaves of England* 1st ed.

Holloway, G. (2005) *Women and work in Britain since 1840* 1st ed. London: Routledge.

Hutchins, B. L. (1907) *Home work and sweating – the causes and remedies* 1st ed. London: Fabian.

Hutchins, B. L. (1915) *Women in modern industry* 1st ed. London: Bell.

Jenkins, Roy. "Dilke, Sir Charles Wentworth, second baronet (1843–1911)." *Oxford Dictionary of National Biography*. Ed. H. C. G. Matthew and Brian Harrison. Oxford: OUP, 2004. Online ed. Ed. Lawrence Goldman. May 2008. 2 Mar. 2010 <http://www.oxforddnb.com/view/article/32824>.

John, A. V. (1980) *By the sweat of their brow – women workers at Victorian coal mines* 1st ed. London:Croom Helm.

John, Angela V. "Tuckwell, Gertrude Mary (1861–1951)." *Oxford Dictionary of National Biography*. Ed. H. C. G. Matthew and Brian Harrison. Oxford: OUP, 2004. Online ed. Ed. Lawrence Goldman. May 2006. 1 Mar. 2010 <http://www.oxforddnb.com/view/article/36572>.

Malone, Carolyn. "Hutchins, Elizabeth Leigh (1858–1935)." *Oxford Dictionary of National Biography*. Ed. H. C. G. Matthew and Brian

Harrison. Oxford: OUP, 2004. Online ed. Ed. Lawrence Goldman. May 2007. 16 Mar. 2010 <http://www.oxforddnb.com/view/article/69834>.

Mallon, J. & Lascelles, E. (1930) *Poverty: Yesterday and to-day* 1st ed. London: Student Christian Movement Press.

Marquand, David. "MacDonald, (James) Ramsay (1866–1937)." *Oxford Dictionary of National Biography*. Ed. H. C. G. Matthew and Brian Harrison. Oxford: OUP, 2004. Online ed. Ed. Lawrence Goldman. Oct. 2009. 16 Mar. 2010 <http://www.oxforddnb.com/view/article/34704>.

Melling, Joseph. "Anderson, William Crawford (1877–1919)." *Oxford Dictionary of National Biography*. Ed. H. C. G. Matthew and Brian Harrison. Oxford: OUP, 2004. Online ed. Ed. Lawrence Goldman. Jan. 2008. 16 Mar. 2010 <http://www.oxforddnb.com/view/article/47322>.

Morgan, C. E. (2001) *Women workers and gender identities, 1835-1913* 1st ed. London: Routledge.

Morgan, Kenneth O. "George, David Lloyd, first Earl Lloyd-George of Dwyfor (1863–1945)." *Oxford Dictionary of National Biography*. Ed. H. C. G. Matthew and Brian Harrison. Oxford: OUP, 2004. Online ed. Ed. Lawrence Goldman. Oct. 2008. 16 Mar. 2010 <http://www.oxforddnb.com/view/article/34570>.

Morgan, Kenneth O. "Hardie, (James) Keir (1856–1915)." *Oxford Dictionary of National Biography*. Ed. H. C. G. Matthew and Brian Harrison. Oxford: OUP, 2004. Online ed. Ed. Lawrence Goldman. May 2007. 16 Mar. 2010 <http://www.oxforddnb.com/view/article/33696>.

Morris, A. J. A. "Gardiner, Alfred George (1865–1946)." *Oxford Dictionary of National Biography*. Ed. H. C. G. Matthew and Brian Harrison. Oxford: OUP, 2004. Online ed. Ed. Lawrence Goldman. May 2006. 16 Mar. 2010 <http://www.oxforddnb.com/view/article/33323>.

Moss, R. (1977) The other side of the chain industry. *Contact* 6 (1) pp.12-13, 17.

Mudie-Smith, R. (1980) *Sweated Industries: A Handbook of the "Daily News" Exhibition*. 2nd ed. London: Garland.

Owen, P (1989) Perceptions of female workers in the Black Country 1870 – 1910 *Journal of the Staffordshire Archeological Society* 13 pp. 1-19.

Pugh, M. (2000) *The march of women* 1st ed. Oxford: OUP.

Smith, H. (2007) *The British women's suffrage campaign, 1866-1928* 2nd ed. London: Pearson Longman.

Taylor, Eric. "Sitch, Charles Henry (1887–1960)." *Oxford Dictionary of National Biography*. Ed. H. C. G. Matthew and Brian Harrison. Oxford: OUP, 2004. 2 Mar. 2010 <http://www.oxforddnb.com/view/article/47381>.

Thom, D. (1998) *Nice Girls and Rude Girls* 1st ed. London: Tauris.

Tuckwell, G. M. & Smith, C. (1908) *Women in industry – from seven points of view* 1st ed. London: Duckworth & Co.

Ward, R. (2005) *City-state and nation – Birmingham's political history* 1st ed. Chichester: Phillimore.

Williams, I. A. "Cadbury, George (1839–1922)." Rev. Robert Fitzgerald. *Oxford Dictionary of National Biography*. Ed. H. C. G. Matthew and Brian Harrison. Oxford: OUP, 2004. Online ed. Ed. Lawrence Goldman. May 2006. 16 Mar. 2010 <http://www.oxforddnb.com/view/article/32232>.

Wrigley, Chris. "Henderson, Arthur (1863–1935)." *Oxford Dictionary of National Biography*. Ed. H. C. G. Matthew and Brian Harrison. Oxford: OUP, 2004. Online ed. Ed. Lawrence Goldman. Jan. 2008. 16 Mar. 2010 <http://www.oxforddnb.com/view/article/33807>.

Newspaper Articles – Chronologically listed

Manchester Dispatch	16.3.1910
Daily Express	22.8.1910
Dundee Courier	23.8.1910
Midland Evening News (Wolverhampton)	23.8.1910
The Daily News	25.8.1910
Express & Star	25.8.1910
Birmingham Dispatch	25.8.1910
Birmingham Mail	26.8.1910
Birmingham Mail	29.8.1910
Birmingham Dispatch	30.8.1910
Evening News	1.9.1910
Birmingham Post	2.9.1910
Birmingham Mail	2.9.1910
The Daily News	5.9.1910
Daily Express	6.9.1910
Birmingham Gazette	6.9.1910
Yorkshire Evening News	6.9.1910
The Daily News	7.9.1910
Birmingham Mail	8.9.1910
Daily Chronicle	10.9.1910
Morning Post	12.9.1910
The Daily News (Midlands edition)	13.9.1910
Wolverhampton Chronicle	14.9.1910

Birmingham Dispatch	16.6.1911
The County Express	17.6.1911
Wolverhampton Chronicle	7.2.1912
Wolverhampton Express & Star	13.7.1913
Evening Mail	22.11.73

Websites

www.visionofbritain.org.uk